INSTINCT

INSTINCT

Rewire Your Brain with Science-
Backed Solutions to Increase
Productivity and Achieve Success

REBECCA HEISS, PHD

CITADEL PRESS
Kensington Publishing Corp.
www.kensingtonbooks.com

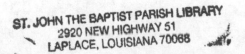

CITADEL PRESS BOOKS are published by

Kensington Publishing Corp.
119 West 40th Street
New York, NY 10018

ISBN-13: 978-0-8065-4103-7
ISBN-10: 0-8065-4103-2

First Citadel hardcover printing: May 2021

10 9 8 7 6 5 4 3 2 1

Printed in the United States of America

Library of Congress Control Number: 2020945318

Electronic edition:

ISBN-13: 978-0-8065-4105-1 (e-book)
ISBN-10: 0-8065-4105-9 (e-book)

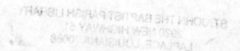

This book is dedicated to the fear(less) dreamer in us all.

Contents

Introduction

OUR BRAINS ARE NOT BUILT for this world. They are built for an environment of scarcity and danger. For over 200,000 years, humans have been developing instinctive behaviors that aligned to help us survive a terribly difficult daily existence. But today, the same instincts that once kept us alive are now preventing us from fully living.

Our world has evolved rapidly in the last two hundred years, through the industrial revolution and subsequent surges in faster technologies, better health, and rising populations. Unfortunately, biology operates on a much slower time scale. As such, our instincts are still operating as if we were in the Stone Age, subconsciously directing us toward possessions we don't need and behaviors that cause us harm in a novel modern environment. For example, our instincts guide us to fear the "other," creating conditions of bias and inequality in the workplace. They push us to viciously compete, rather than cooperate, with our colleagues. Our primitive directives even compel us to cheat in order to vanquish perceived competitors, causing unnecessary havoc at home and at work. It doesn't have to be that way. We can consciously begin making changes—now.

The goal of this book is to help you: (1) develop awareness of an instinct at play and how it is mismatched to the current environment; (2) recognize the outcome that said instinct is trying to achieve; and (3) use the instinct interventions provided in this book to nudge the alignment of your actions, beliefs, and experiences in order to achieve the positive outcome *intended*. To be clear: Instincts are not bad. They just aren't necessarily good either. Instincts aren't meant to be moralized in any one way. It's the *outcomes* that result from these instincts that, depending upon the unique circumstances, prove to be positive or negative.

Thanks to millions of years of evolution, our brains are amazing at recognizing danger and instantaneously responding in ways that keep us safe before we are even conscious of what is happening. Fear is at the root of our survival. Fear kept our ancestors safe from predators and competitors, while driving our instincts to hunt, gather, and find eligible mates. Fear is that snap of your hand off the stove before you even realized that it was hot. It's that chill down your spine and the quickening of your pace seconds before you noticed the stranger in the alley.

But the problem is that our brains are still operating under ancient programming that doesn't always serve us in a modern environment. Haunted by the biological ghosts of our ancestors, our minds still rely on outdated instinctual responses that ultimately cause us a lot of pain, suffering, and unhappiness.

Maybe you're not convinced that your brain still believes that you live in the Stone Age? That's not surprising, given that one of our core instincts is to self-delude (the focus of Chapter 4), but for now, consider this: The top three things Americans say they fear most are public speaking; heights; and bugs, snakes, or similar animals. Our stress levels spike through the roof just thinking about talking to an audience, peering over a ledge, or seeing a creature slither in the grass. And that makes sense if you're a caveperson who knows that ostracism from your tribe, a steep cliff, or a venomous bite can all result in fatal consequences. But the last time I checked, nobody's ever died from giving a TED Talk and the chances of you stepping on a venomous snake as you wander through the grocery store parking lot are next to zero.

In fact, the number one killer of Americans is heart disease. About 1 in 4 of us will die from it. So, shouldn't our sophisticated brains be terrified of Ben & Jerry's ice cream? Shouldn't our heart rate soar at the sight of a Big Mac? Shouldn't we embrace our workouts with a passion that matches our fear of extinction? Sadly, just the opposite is true. Our brains *crave* the very foods that threaten our lives. Our ancestral minds *hate* expending energy on exercise. Why? Because conservation of energy and increased consumption of fats and sugars were key to our survival, especially in times of scarcity. In order to counter our maladaptive behaviors we need first to recognize we are behaving from a subconscious *instinct* rather than a conscious *choice*.

Why are we resorting to instincts? Because the overwhelming amount of input received by our brains requires that most data are passed directly to the faster-processing subconscious. The reality of living in a technologically advanced society of 8 billion, globally connected individuals is that today, on average, our brains are charged with the task of processing over *400 billion* bits of information every second! This task seems impossible until recognizing that the average brain comprises 80 billion individual neurons (cells), making tens of thousands of connections to other brain cells. There are as many neurons in that four-pound brain in your head as there are stars in the Milky Way galaxy. But our conscious minds operate slowly and intentionally. We are only consciously aware of (and able to consciously process) a limited amount of data. With so much happening up there, most of our brains' dealings are done behind the wall of the subconscious.

Claremont Graduate University's Distinguished Professor of Psychology and Management Mihaly Csikszentmihalyi and renowned engineer and inventor Robert Lucky both independently estimated that the *conscious* mind has the capacity to process data at about 120 bits per second. To put that into perspective, we process about 60 bits per second of information when we consciously pay attention to a single person talking to us. Give us two people to pay attention to and we are at capacity. When you do the math, it makes sense that neuroscientists suggest that we live 95 to 99 percent of our lives in a subconscious state. That means up to 99 percent of the time you are unaware of your emotions, behaviors, and decisions—let alone what drives them! That should be a startling and disturbing realization. When it comes to engaging our brains to override our instincts, we haven't gotten much further than our Stone Age ancestors—despite the fact that we are equipped with the brain power to do so.

Our pre-programmed instincts set us up for a subconscious existence because critical thinking in the midst of danger was not only uncalled for, it could be downright fatal. Imagine processing the many components of how to respond to a lion attack. Our brains developed shortcuts (such as the fight-or-flight-or-freeze response) to handle such situations. But where does that leave us in a modern environment? How do our brains respond when we need to be critically processing information that is essential to the survival of our businesses? Or our relationships? The danger has been reversed: Our instincts drive us to respond without the careful consideration and critical thinking these challenges demand, resulting in unintended loss in our productivity and success.

The good news is that we are not powerless. Our brains are highly malleable. We can train our subconscious to better react. Our brains are also incredibly adept. No other animal on earth has the expanded frontal lobe that humans exhibit, giving us the unique capability to implement executive control over our behaviors. In my work, both as a CEO and as a biologist, I've had the privilege of helping a wide range of clients and audiences seeking strategies to live more fearless, productive, and self-directed lives. This book is meant to be a guide—your training plan. It will help you to rise above the old, ingrained habits that no longer serve you and enhance your ability to become your best biological self.

Across the next seven chapters, I will provide you with advice and insights that will help you to intervene in outdated instincts. In Chapter 1, we'll explore the most primal instinct of all: "Survival." And we'll examine how our instinctual brains keep us locked into fear rather than relaxed in flow. But with a few clear interventions, you'll learn how to keep up in a fast-paced world by first *slowing down*. In Chapter 2, "Sex," we'll investigate the ways in which gender roles differ biologically. And I'll reveal how one specific policy missing from most workplace sexual harassment handbooks has the capacity to save your company millions of dollars. Chapter 3, "Variety," looks at the reasons why less truly is more. Amid a world of seemingly endless choices, our instinct to crave *variety* leaves us restless and unsatisfied. But I'll arm you with interventions that shift your brain's perspective to fulfillment without compromising your drive. Chapter 4 focuses on "Self-Deception," an instinct that was a lifesaver for our ancestors, and yet today it comes at a great personal and professional cost. But here, I'll provide simple hacks that help you to recognize the harmful lies we tell ourselves, and emerge better prepared to see the world more consciously. You'll also discover how recognizing and intervening in this instinct can make the difference between success and failure. Chapter 5, "Belonging," reveals one of our most powerful primal directives. You'll see how, in an environment that pushes us to compete, cooperation actually serves us all much better—whether in groups or as individuals. Chapter 6 explores how easily our "Fear of the Other" influences decisions that ultimately lead to detrimental practices. I'll give you simple steps to actively seek out discomfort and train your brain to stay in a more conscious, less-stressed space, in order to make the most creative and accurate decisions. Finally, Chapter 7, "Information Gathering," examines why our days feel so full but our tanks are still empty. Despite the fact that our instinct to gather facts leads us to consume more data and information than ever before, we still find ourselves missing key information and falling out of touch with the needs of our clients, friends, and families.

We can thank our ancestral brains for helping us to achieve peerless success as a species. But as evolved human beings, it's time for us to take charge of ourselves. Thankfully, we all possess the power to begin reframing our instincts for the new world. This book provides you with the knowledge and skills to identify, intervene, and optimize your own instincts. It will arm you with straightforward interventions that *work with your biology, rather than against it*. By the end of the book, you will begin to make better decisions at work, at home, and in all of your relationships. And you can begin to live a more fully conscious life.

INSTINCT

Survival

Making Haste, Slowly

I WAS FREEZING. LITERALLY, FREEZING. Soaked head to toe with the icy waters of the Hudson River, I knew I was in trouble. I was blowing into my hands, my breath the only remaining source of warmth in my body. But soon even that began to come out of me cold. I don't remember much after that, just a blur of numbing, stinging, icy-hot sensations along my skin as I slipped into hypothermia.

The day had started as an adventure. My father and I were rafting along the Hudson River for our annual father-daughter trip. There were icicles hanging on the trees overhead; a late snow dusted the branches. I'd always wanted to go whitewater rafting, so Dad chose the *best* time for it—the first day of the season, when the rapids were running fast. My dad knows that if there's a possibility for speed, I want the *top* speed. But on this day, the first of April, the weather was unseasonably cold . . . even by New York standards.

We'd come prepared in our wetsuits and, at the start of the day, I was feeling optimistic and undeterred by the rapidly falling temperature. Then, about an hour into the trip, I experienced the first signs of hypothermia: I lost feeling in my extremities. Everything in me started to feel heavy, and the world around me began to move in slow motion—especially my own body. I looked back at my dad smiling and paddling at the rear of the raft. I looked ahead and determined we had another hour before we'd make it to shore, to warmth and safety. I couldn't think myself out of this situation. Even if I told my dad that I was in trouble, he'd be as helpless as I was to do anything. And that's when my survival instinct took full control, sending a rush of blessed warmth from between my legs down to my feet.

My body had ceased paying attention to social niceties. It wanted to live and it would do whatever it needed to ensure survival—including constricting my blood vessels to keep warmth around my essential internal organs, thereby forcing my kidneys to keep pace with my rapidly increasing blood pressure. I was sixteen, and I had just urinated all over myself. Honestly, I was too cold to even care. Survival instincts had completely taken over my bodily response.

Human beings are adept at creating constructs that enforce civil behavior. But those constructs go out the window when our survival instinct is activated. Urinating on oneself, for example, is suddenly a viable option when we are under duress.

Our survival instinct kicks in strong in order to drown out "should" or "shouldn't" voices in our heads. We just take action. Consciously or not. Thank goodness, because (spoiler alert!) I'm still alive because of it. Once back to shore, Dad quickly got me in front of a fully stoked fireplace that relieved my body from threat.

In this situation, my survival instinct got to work by conserving heat. But in other scenarios, this instinct can lessen your disgust response to, say, eating the family dog for sustenance (a sad reality for hiker Marco Lavoie who, in 2013, was forced to eat his beloved German shepherd after being stranded for months without supplies in the Canadian wilderness). A strong survival instinct can even reduce pain receptors that would otherwise prevent you from amputating your own arm—just as Aron Ralston, the subject of the movie *127 Hours*, discovered. If you've ever consumed a stupid amount of alcohol, you can thank your survival instinct for shutting down your behavior by putting you into an unconscious state, vomiting the poison, or both.

Survival is at the root of all the other instincts you'll learn about in this book. It is powerful and deeply written into our subconscious. You can easily witness this if you were to intentionally try to harm yourself. (But please don't! I'm not advocating this behavior, just illustrating a point.) One of my favorite urban myths is the idea that we could bite through our fingers as easily as a carrot if our brain didn't stop us from doing so. Despite the fact that it's not true (it takes a *lot* more force), it does provide a sense of how our instincts really are trying to protect us from our, admittedly, dumb ideas.

A better example of your survival instinct in action is when you accidentally put your hand on a hot stove and your brain quickly and reflexively directs you to remove it. But here's the cool part: That movement away from the source of danger occurs *before* your brain has time to process what happened: The pain receptors are activated before you are consciously aware of the pain. In other words, your instinct is driving your behavior before you fully comprehend the reason.

When our Stone Age ancestors felt stress, the survival instinct came racing to the rescue because stressors back then—say, a tiger about to pounce or impending starvation—were often life threatening. But here's the problem: Our survival-primed brain is overextending itself. In a modern context, that tiger becomes Joseph the accountant wondering where your financial reports are, or Kathy the CEO wondering when you'll get back to her on that email she sent you a *full* two minutes ago. The same survival instinct that served you so well in the wild is responding to everyday stressors as if they were full-out, life-threatening events. There is a mismatch in our modern brains. Our fears and discomforts today no longer mean that we are in immediate danger.

We will explore this disconnect more in depth when we examine the stress reaction, but suffice it to say that most of the stressors we encounter daily are not life threatening. So why does our body react if they are? Why can't our brain differentiate between real threats and perceived threats? The answer is that our survival instinct is running the show far beyond the value of its contribution.

We still need this instinct (think about the last tIme you got out of the way of an oncoming vehicle *just* in time), but we need to learn to better control it. Otherwise, survival can cause lasting damage to our health and our relationships, and even lead us to miss life's most beautiful moments.

The Street Performer

One day in January 2017, at 7:51 a.m., a man in jeans and a ball cap set up a post along a busy hub of the Washington, D.C., metro and began to play his violin. He left the instrument's case open by his feet, should one of the hundreds of commuters passing by care to reward his efforts.

For forty-three minutes, masterfully crafted music poured from his violin—agonizingly beautiful strains of Bach, Massenet, Schubert, and Ponce that had moved concertgoers to their feet in halls across the world. But they went mostly unnoticed here. None of the people who were rushing by seemed to know that they were turning a deaf ear to internationally acclaimed virtuoso Joshua Bell, who was performing on one of the most valuable violins ever made, a 1713 Stradivarius.

A child prodigy, Bell had sold out symphony halls, played to standing-room-only crowds, and commanded prices of up to $1,000 per minute. But standing there on the subway platform, looking much like a beggar, his melodies fell on deaf ears. People hustled past. Busy. Late for wherever they were rushing to—perhaps, ironically, so they could get off early enough to get highly sought-after tickets to one of Bell's concerts.

Bell left with only the few dollars that had been hurriedly tossed into his case. Of the 1,070 people who walked past, just seven took in his performance for longer than a minute, and most of them were children. The majority of commuters didn't even bother to look up from their programmed march.

What does this say about us as a society? *Washington Post* reporter Gene Weingarten, who originally covered this story, summed it up perfectly: "If we can't take the time out of our lives to stay a moment and listen to one of the best musicians on Earth play some of the best music ever written; if the surge of modern life so overpowers us that we are deaf and blind to something like that—then what else are we missing?"

What else are you missing because you are too busy to stop and pay attention? What pleasures are drained by the stress of everyday life? And why are we overlooking

the beautiful overtures in our abundant, modern environment? I believe our instincts are to blame.

Ironically, even among those who can afford to pay
$1,000 per minute for music, fly in private jets, and *choose*
what they want to eat—rather than being grateful to have
anything to eat—their brains are still stuck in a cycle of
survival. Daily existence in the modern world has forced
us into a perpetual state of busy that persisted even in the
midst of stay-at-home orders. We tend to view *time* as a
precious and scarce resource, as if there were never
enough hours in the day to get everything done. Why is
that? Technological advances in the last two hundred
years, from washing machines to Uber Eats, afford us
more free time than ever, yet we lull ourselves into the il-
lusion that we have less time.

Consider your daily routine. Maybe you woke up this
morning to the blaring beeps of your alarm, drank a
steamy cup of stimulants, and then huddled up against
strangers on a crowded train platform or spent the morning behind the wheel of your car jammed in traffic. You
rushed into the office or onto your Zoom call just after 9
a.m., hoping no one would notice you were a few minutes late. You spent your day communicating with
strangers, doing what you could to interpret signals
(often without the benefit of a face or tone of voice). You
left work at 6 p.m., feeling anxious for all that's still on
your plate, and the reports you never got around to. You
picked up your kids at day care, thanking the strangers
you've entrusted your most precious assets to all day.

Then, your in-laws call: They're coming over for a surprise visit! What's for dinner? Finally, after everyone else is asleep, you lie in bed doom-scrolling mindlessly through social media to make sure you're not missing out on important updates. By the time your head hits the pillow it's nearly midnight. Notifications from your phone stir you as you toss and turn in bed for the next six hours. The blaring alarm starts the cycle all over again.

Writing that paragraph actually elicited a bit of a stress response for me, and I was just *writing* it. Stress used to be a life-saving stimulus that triggered our fight-or-flight-or-freeze response—a behavior that pushes us to fight a predator, run to safety, or hunker down and hope to go unnoticed. But our brains are lousy at interpreting the difference between real and perceived threats. A real threat, for instance, is a hungry tiger jumping into your bedroom at night. Not likely to happen in a modern environment. But that doesn't stop our brains from "protecting" us from threats it *perceives,* and triggering the fight-flight-freeze response in inappropriate circumstances, like when we're around people who are different from us, or when we're stuck in a particularly nasty traffic jam, or when we hear the sound of dinging emails that require immediate attention. Externally, our lives are far safer and easier than those of our ancestors, but our survival-obsessed brains act as if we've encountered one hundred tigers by lunchtime! Our brains are experiencing a different reality altogether.

The result is that our brains stay locked in survival mode, preventing us from experiencing or lingering in pleasurable moments, like the sound of violins in the subway station or the smell of freshly baked bread wafting out of a bakery. Pleasure is secondary to survival. So we scope out the "danger" all around us, certain that there's not enough time for "luxurious" activities. But missing the most precious moments of life is not the only downside of our out-of-date instincts. Our health and performance take serious hits as well.

Stressing the Effects of Stress on Health and Performance

Stress has been called the "health epidemic of the 21st century." Why is this? Let's look at what happens when your body goes into a fight-flight-freeze response and a cascade of hormonal reactions occur. First, adrenaline is released, giving you that immediate shaky, sweaty hands, pumping heart, super strength. Adrenaline is a powerful, but short-lived, neurotransmitter, because in nature, real-life battles don't last very long. Either you escape the tiger or you're its meal. Adrenaline is very useful in those first precious seconds after a threat is detected, but then cortisol, the main stress hormone, is quickly called in to assist in sustaining the fight-flight-freeze response, and to repair any damage you sustained during the threat.

Cortisol's most important function is to break down proteins and give you quick access to glucose, the fuel currency of the body. During a stressful experience, glucose provides immediate energy to the major muscles to assist you in fighting or fleeing the situation. It provides energy to combat trauma, illness, and infection. Similarly useful is cortisol's suppression of the immune, reproductive, and digestive systems, all of which are nonessential in the stressed state. Imagine if in the middle of a fight for your life, you were suddenly sexually aroused or hungry. These distractions are completely eliminated, compliments of your adrenal system binding cortisol to receptors in your brain that regulate the behaviors.

All of these intricate components work together in a miraculous, choreographed dance to keep you safe from harm without your ever having to consciously sound an alarm. But here is perhaps the biggest biological flaw that has revealed itself in modern times: the failure of our stress response to adapt to and differentiate modern stressors from truly life-threatening stressors.

In our ancestral environment, this cascade of responses was a short-term and rarely elicited solution. Modern life, however, constantly bombards us with sensory input at speeds we simply cannot process. As a result, we often find ourselves in a condition of sensory overload, causing our brains to perceive *everything* as stressful in order to "keep us safe."

Ironically, this over-sensitization puts us in a dangerous state of chronic stress. Chronic stress differs from the acute stressors your body was built to handle in that you never fully get a reprieve from the surge of cortisol. During an acute stress response, your cortisol levels shoot up until the threat has passed and then return to normal within about an hour. With repeated, nearly continuous exposure to stressors in a modern environment, our cortisol levels are constantly being stimulated, resulting in new, higher baseline norms, with potentially devastating consequences.

We know, for example, that chronically elevated cortisol levels depress the immune system, leaving you prone to illness. Corporate America endures significant costs associated with illness-related absenteeism—an estimated annual price tag of $1,900 per employee according to research by John Hancock, on top of health care costs that are 46 percent higher for stressed employees relative to their less-stressed counterparts, according to the National Institute for Occupational Safety and Health. So it's no surprise that the state of stress (including the mental, physical, and psychological costs) during the COVID-19 pandemic skyrocketed. Approximately 88 percent of workers reported "moderate to extreme stress," in an April 2020 survey, with 62 percent saying they lost "at least 1 hour a day in productivity," and 32 percent "at least 2 hours a day" due to pandemic-related stress. Ironically, their stress leaves these workers more immunologically vulnerable to illness.

The American Psychological Association links chronic stress to the six leading causes of death: heart disease, cancer, lung ailments, accidents, cirrhosis of the liver, and suicide. Stress can even prematurely age us! Studies show that chronic stress is associated with shorter telomeres, the protective caps of your chromosomes that affect how your cells age. Telomeres are akin to the plastic ends of shoelaces—they keep everything from fraying. But as cortisol levels rise, telomeres unravel causing more rapid aging. Along with the quickened aging process, elevated cortisol decreases brain-derived neurotrophic factor, a protein that protects your brain cells. Raised cortisol has even been implicated in lowered IQ. When your body endures stress, it turns on stem cells in the brain that inhibit connections to your prefrontal cortex (where most of your higher-level cognitive processing occurs).

A 2018 study published in *Neurology* linked higher cortisol to poorer performance on tests of memory, organization, and attention. Within a sample of over two thousand asymptomatic middle-age workers, the subjects with the highest cortisol levels were also more likely to have physical changes in their brains consistent with early markers of Alzheimer's disease. But our health isn't the only concern. Our performance at work suffers as well.

Separate peer-reviewed scientific studies published in 2003 and 2015 found that the administration of cortisol to artificially induce stress impaired the subject's ability to detect errors while simultaneously increased their appetite for risk. It's hard to imagine a worse recipe for workplace disaster. Participants in a 2016 study were asked to solve math problems aloud at increasingly rapid inter-

vals, with harsh buzzes sounded when they answered in-
correctly. The stressed subjects suffered significant
decreases in such executive functions as attention and in-
hibition, task management, planning, and coding.

Our work and our health suffer when we are stressed.
A stressed-out brain creates a vicious cycle, causing you
to stay locked in survival mode. But you can break free of
stressful interpretations by using your higher cognitive
powers to make better choices.

Just Enough Time . . . to Make a Poor Decision

Survival is like an internal bodyguard, poised to pounce
into action swiftly and efficiently whenever it detects a
threat. Having a bodyguard is a great thing. But in this
case, that guard is often misguided, overworked, and consistently setting off false alarm bells, causing you to react
before thinking—even in non-life-threatening situations.

We can't bring our best thinking to a problem when
we let our survival instinct lead and influence our decision-making. Cue the memory of the instinctive
reaction you had to the last recession, when you liqui-
dated your investment portfolio. Or that time you
stormed off, threatening to quit, after you were skipped
over for a promotion you deserved. Or the time when
you were feeling particularly emotional, started packing
in Ben & Jerry's, and before you knew it, you'd devoured
the entire pint. You guessed it. That's your survival

instinct at work. Fighting, fleeing, and freezing in these non-life-threatening situations.

From your internal bodyguard's perspective, it's better to have you covered . . . *just in case*. As a result, we are too eager to react without first understanding or questioning the source of danger. Maybe it's nothing more than a bumpy financial period, or time for a conversation with the boss about why we were passed over, or a feeling of sadness that will pass. Instead of using our executive functioning, we make decisions from the reactionary portion of our minds, reaching premature conclusions to resolve the situation *quickly,* rather than in the best manner we could.

A dear friend has a saying: "If you want it bad, you'll get it bad. Good things take time." What she means is this: If we want something badly, we are often liable to take shortcuts, resulting in us getting that thing—but likely a bad version of it. If our brains want us to survive (badly), sometimes what we get as a result isn't the best. If we don't get a chance to process situations before our instincts take over in *actual* life-threatening situations, what hope do we have for the rest of our lives?

Thankfully, most of us are not making *actual* life-or-death decisions on a day-to-day basis. But once again, our brains are bad at interpreting real from perceived threats. Too frequently this means that we fall back to our survival instincts in search of a quick, black-and-white response—because that's how our instincts were designed. Black and white. Life and death. But relying on binary judgments is a disastrous way to operate in a world of gray, tangled, and complex decisions. Our ability to make good decisions degrades under stress, largely as a result of two mechanisms:

1. A narrowing or premature closure of the decision-making process that leads to all options either not being evaluated or not being evaluated carefully enough before a decision is made;
2. An unsystematic scan in which the review of options available goes from being logical to frantic or disorganized, often feeding back into a biased resolution.

Imagine, for instance, that your boss has asked you to select food for the big company party. You are responsible for feeding five hundred people, and the event is in one week. What do you do? Maybe a quick Google search to find a local, mid-range, generic catering service. If you're really under the gun, you'll probably bias your search to restaurants or menus from which you've previously eaten. Will you consider looking at companies that may not be listed on Google or Yelp? Will you do the research it would take to realize that the party is going to be outside and might better be served by a slew of food trucks? Will you take into consideration that there's an unlimited budget, so flying in lobsters from Maine is not only a good idea, but the *best* option? Given the time

constraints, you probably didn't even consider food al-
lergies, or the fact that a quarter of the employees are
vegetarians, or, or, or...

Now imagine that the dinner is in two hours and your
job is on the line.

Time is arguably our greatest, self-imposed stressor. It
further compresses our exploration of creative alternatives. In this scenario, you might get so overwhelmed
that you just book anything. Or maybe your instincts opt
for the freeze mode and you're unable to make any decisions. In today's market, the pressure to innovate and
iterate quickly is overwhelming. Rather than taking the
time when we need to on the front end to slow down and
evaluate the situation, we race to a solution. I liken this
to trying to carry water from a well with a bucket full of
holes. We are so anxious to complete the task of fetching
water that we never pause long enough to fix the bucket
we are carrying it in, so that the task can be done with
more efficiency.

Within this space of constant pressure, classically
poor decisions are made. I personally have fallen into
this trap on numerous occasions. My business partner
and I joke that his survival instinct is freeze: He designs
fifteen different varieties of buckets with various fixes but
never actually implements any of them. Meanwhile, I'm
racing back and forth from the well with six buckets, all
leaking, and no plan.

Recently, while developing an app project, my survival instinct nearly led us to disaster. During beta testing,

our app received great feedback, but I felt overwhelmed. In survival mode, I began passing along hundreds of comments, patches, bugs, features, and ideas (some directly conflicting with others) to our development team. As soon as the team would move in one direction, my instructions would pivot us to another. Meanwhile, my partner was designing plans as fast as he could, only for them to be irrelevant by day's end. It soon became obvious what was happening: Our survival instincts were keeping us in the weeds. We had to slow down to speed up. Once we took the time to analyze all the feedback together, a clear path forward emerged. He designed a logical plan and I got it implemented. Before long, the team was on the same page and moving forward together with greater speed than before.

Falling to our survival instincts can even affect how we respond to the fallout of our choices. In 2013, a line of yoga pants released by athletic wear company Lululemon was inadvertently made with sheer material that left some women more exposed than they cared to be. Sales plummeted and pants were recalled from shelves to the tune of an estimated $67 million hit to sales. That's when company CEO Chip Wilson told a TV reporter that "some women's bodies just don't actually work," for Lululemon pants. Not only did he come off as derogatory toward a large subset of women, he exposed the company's lack of consideration in making wise product decisions for this population.

Poor life decisions are driven quite regularly by our faulty survival instinct. Take, for example, the story of a man we'll call "Bob." Bob is a CEO of a mid-size company that has been successful for over fifty years. But recently, Bob's leadership has fallen under criticism. The company's revenues are in decline and Bob has failed to adjust to massively shifting markets. Several suggestions have been made by the team, notably a plan brought forth by another member of the executive team, Steve. While the team strongly supported Steve's initiative, Bob has publicly called it "weak, and impossible to employ." Despite intense discussions with the board and strong analytical support for Steve's plan, Bob refuses to implement it.

Why would Bob make such a lousy decision? Because he was feeling pressure beyond that of the business. In fact, he compounded his poor decision with a physical altercation. On the same day his company reported its biggest loss to date, Bob turned a corner in his office and bumped into Steve, knocking himself over in the process. Embarrassed and flustered, he reacted by jumping to his feet and shoving Steve, throwing loud verbal assaults at the bewildered executive.

While Bob's terrible reaction was obviously misdirected (and frankly the recipe for a lawsuit!), it provides us with a classic illustration of the survival instinct. To Bob, Steve is a rival—a challenge to his status and position in the company. Ancestrally, challenges to a leader meant life or death. Removing rivals and maintaining a reputation for solid leadership conferred massive biological benefits. But if a leader let their guard down, others might devalue their leadership position. Traditionally, usurpers of power rarely took the risk of leaving former leaders alive. Of course, Bob *consciously* knew that his life wasn't being threatened. But that didn't stop his faulty survival instinct from driving poor life choices.

When life, or our company's future, feels unsteady or unsure, our brains kick into a reactionary state. We've all had those "open mouth, insert foot" moments that surely Wilson experienced immediately after his statement on Lululemon's pants. We've all lashed out at would-be rivals or run away from an issue rather than addressing it head on. Stress doesn't affect only the weak or those who "can't handle the workload." It shakes us all, and it's high time we woke up with a better response.

Relativity and a Distracted World

How do we get our brains to allow us the time to make the best decisions? *To rewire your survival instinct, you're going to have to bend time.*

Remember that time is a human construct. As such, its perception by any individual can be manipulated by a number of factors. When Einstein first published his Theory of Relativity, his secretary was so overwhelmed with reporters asking her to explain the theory that Einstein reportedly gave her the following summary to parrot: "When you sit with a nice girl for two hours you think it's only a minute, but when you sit on a hot stove for a minute you think it's two hours. That's relativity."

What I suppose Einstein meant is that time is relative. We experience it differently depending upon the context. The more we can learn how to control how we experience time, the better decisions we can make independent of the stressor in the moment. Time perception is often described in two forms: a retrospective and a prospective experience.

A *retrospective* experience of time is how we interpret time that has already happened. Our recall of the past. *Prospective* time, on the other hand, is when you look forward: What's coming down the pipeline? What does our day hold? What is the next emergency we are going to have to clean up? When we are feeling busy, always looking to the next task, time flies by. We never feel like we have enough of it to accomplish what we need. Ideally, we'd all be capable of staying in the present moment for the majority of our experiences, but too easily our minds slip toward worrying about the future or ruminating on the past.

Ironically, technology contributes to this time-stressed feeling. Psychologist Aoife McLoughlin has demonstrated through multiple studies that our addiction to technology has an unexpected time cost. When we are regularly checking our social media feeds and text messages, we think that time is passing faster than it is. Our perception of time speeds up! We've likely all had this experience when our intentions are to only check our phones for a brief minute, and when we look up, we've lost half an hour. Additional research finds that when we *believe* there's insufficient time to complete a task, we perform much worse—even if we actually have plenty of time. Taken in conjunction, our addiction to technology has created an environment in which our brain perceives time scarcity, and as a result we fail to perform at our highest levels.

Georgetown University professor Cal Newport addresses this challenge in his book *Deep Work: Rules for Focused Success in a Distracted World*, in which he emphasizes the dire need for us all to find ways to move away from shallow work. Shallow work, Newport says, includes "non-cognitively demanding, logistical-style tasks, often performed while distracted. These efforts tend to not create new value in the world and are easy to replicate." Think: email, text messages, social posts. Turns out, the five seconds you decide to take to quickly scan an incoming message doesn't just cost you five seconds. It actually costs you about twenty-three *minutes* (twenty-three minutes and fifteen seconds to be exact) on average to return your full focus back to your original task. Gloria Mark's empirical study that first uncovered this massive time cost also found that interrupted workers then tried to compensate for the time lost by working faster, leading to more stress, frustration, and effort for lowered productivity. The subjects in this study (and maybe you and your colleagues) all need a little *festina lente*.

Festina lente is a Latin phrase that translates to "make haste, slowly." We've all heard the "slow down to speed up" adage, but in a world that's spinning ever faster, slowing down seems like a sure way to lose the race. The key to helping your survival instinct work with you rather than against you lies in *festina lente. Fix the bucket before you race to fetch more water.*

Believing to Achieve— Bending Time to Your Advantage

To better focus on deep work—those cognitively challenging issues that demand your full attention—it can help to batch shallow work activities into specific time chunks. For example, you do emails only from 7 a.m. to 8 a.m., 12 p.m. to 1 p.m., and 4 p.m. to 5 p.m., rather than trying to process each message as it comes in. The more we can train our brains to stay present with a single task, the stronger our performance.

A University of California–Irvine study demonstrated that the average worker switches tasks about every three minutes. Another study found that 70 percent of emails are opened within six seconds of receipt. All these technological interruptions turn our brains into sieves, unable to retain concentration. And, according to a study from Carnegie Mellon, they lower our ability to answer questions correctly by about 20 percent!

Imagine for a moment that you scheduled time without technological interruptions, and blocked out space for deep work. What if you believed with certainty that you had enough time to accomplish everything you need to accomplish? How would you behave differently?

How can you behave as if you have enough time, when your brain is telling you that you don't? You simply have to slow down your brain to gain the *experience* of more time. When you don't have a lot of stimuli engaging your brain, time seems to pass more slowly. The last five minutes of deep work can feel as if it was thirty minutes judging by your level of productive output. It turns out we have a lot of control over our perspective of time.

"The brain goes through a lot of trouble to edit and present a story to you of what's going on out there and how fast or slowly it happens," explains Stanford University neuroscientist David Eagleman. "What your brain's telling you [that] you see is not always what's out there. It's trying to put together the best, most useful story of what's happening in the world." In other words: The key is to helm the editing desk of your own brain and tell it the story you want to be telling: You have enough time.

My friend and mentor Artie Isaac keeps a Post-it note stuck to his computer screen, which reads, "This is your captain speaking." It's a reminder to communicate to his team the same way the captain of a plane might communicate to her passengers: calm, clear, unrushed. We all should apply this idea to our brain's editing room, so that we tell stories that are more effective in a modern environment. "Hey brain, this is your captain speaking. I know you're trying to piece together a story that's useful for me, but it would be so much better if we edited this film like *this* instead. Cut this. Keep that."

We can see more clearly how our brains edit meaning-ful stories for us when we take a moment to recall where we were on 9/11. Or when Kennedy was shot. Or what song was on the radio when you crashed that car. Most of us have vivid memories of highly emotionally charged situations because our brains are recording as much de-tail as possible in these scenarios. In case you survive a crisis situation, your brain has a clear story about how to direct your behaviors the next time something similar happens. It creates a highlight reel with lots of "footage" to refer back to. And the more data you have around an event, the longer you interpret it taking.

I call this the *Matrix Effect*, after the famously slow-motion action scenes in the 1999 movie when the hero discovered he could simply bend away from a formidable force of bullets careening toward him. How can we use the Matrix Effect to our advantage? We have to learn to intentionally slow down time *in the moment.*

Better Call Sully:
Slowing Time in the Moment

Who better to look to for training in this arena than people who regularly move through danger with calm and con-trol? For most of us, when we experience a real-life emergency, like being trapped in a raging fire, or terrorized by a mass shooter, our survival instincts kick in for good reason. But what about if you're a firefighter? Or a member of an emergency room medical team? What allows some people to override their instincts and run directly toward a threat? These experts in their respective fields have trained extensively and continuously to equip themselves to approach life-and-death situations with a control that goes far beyond the survival instinct most of us have.

Consider Captain "Sully" Sullenberger's reaction when his Airbus craft struck a flock of Canada geese and lost power to both engines. Sully didn't have time to survey all of his choices or consult experts in his field about the pros and cons of the decision he was about to make. He had to react quickly. With surprising calm and speed he negotiated his options and ultimately landed the plane safely on the Hudson River. He credits his success to years of training. Sully had plenty of time. He'd been in that simulator running the scenario thousands of times before. His brain had recorded plenty of footage.

"For 42 years," he said, "I've been making small, regular deposits in this bank of experience, education, and training. And on January 15, the balance was sufficient so that I could make a very large withdrawal."

Sully's 19,663 flight hours and repetitive training allowed this life-or-death decision to be processed efficiently and automatically in the moment. But what about those of us who aren't facing life-threatening decisions every day, but whose brains are being triggered as if we were? How do *we* cope?

Firefighters, emergency room team members, and captains of airplanes all have very specific scenarios for which they train, for thousands of hours, so they can expertly handle that moment everyone hopes will never come. And nearly all their training begins the same way: *Take a breath and assess the situation*. We can train our survival instincts to relax, allowing us to think logically in the face of the unpredictable challenges we encounter every day, by adopting the same strategy and slowing time.

Let's look at the passengers aboard Sully's plane. Their brains were recording an enormous amount of footage from that harrowing experience. As a result, if they were to retrospectively recall the incident, the scenario would feel as if it took an eternity to play out. In reality the plane was airborne at 3:25 p.m., struck a flock of birds two minutes later, and lost both engines immediately. Sully made a mayday call before he put the plane in the Hudson. From the mayday call to impact, the incident lasted only ninety seconds. That's half the time we spend brushing our teeth! And although retrospectively, the passengers felt like the drama lasted hours, on the plane that day, they likely felt as if the whole event happened rather quickly.

"In the blink of the eye" and "it all happened so fast!" is not uncommon to hear from witnesses immediately following a traumatic event. It's only later, when the brain has processed all the footage, that we look back and get the time-expansion experience. So what if you consciously took control of a stressful experience *in the moment*? What if you used time expansion to alleviate your day-to-day cortisol-raising moments?

Here's the Action: Bend Time by Doing Something Novel, *Consciously*

While our perception of time slips away from us with regular interruptions, we can help control time by pulling our attention to our present moment. For example, the next time you're in a traffic jam, count the red cars, put on a song you never play, create your own sauna by blasting the heat, or car-dance and encourage the person next to you to do the same. Engage in a "first." It doesn't have to be epic or heart-pounding. Just do something different enough to spark your brain into "recording" mode. The goal is to be super-conscious of the recording your brain is doing *as it's happening*.

For anyone who is a second child, you're probably aware of the upshot of novelty. For example, your parents took at least three times as many photos of your older sibling's childhood moments, relative to yours. It's not because they love him more, it's just that everything their first child did was novel to them. Your parents were so excited!

Look! David is walking!
Look! David's first bath!
Look! David took a poop in the middle of the floor!

Do I sound bitter? I'm not. I swear I'm perfectly happy being the second, less-novel child. It could have been a lot worse—I could have been third!

The point is your brain operates *exactly* like the parents of later-born children. Been there, done that. No reason to hit the record button again.

To better control your brain, you just have to engage in something unique enough that your brain sits up and pays attention: *Oh! That's different. I should record some footage of this.* As you engage in these novel bursts, your old neural patterns get interrupted. The day-to-day blur of high cortisol injections and the monotonous script of "it's a big scary world out there" get derailed. Like a loud commercial break when you've fallen asleep to the drones of a late-night television program, novelty shakes you awake to a more conscious state and your brain takes notice.

Some of us (read: me) need help with this. So a simple hack I use is to set alarms throughout my day that remind me to do something novel to slow down time (make sure these are scheduled to go off outside of the time you've allotted for deep work!). When your alarm goes off, put down the phone, step away from the computer, or disengage from whatever you are busy with. A helpful way to start is to check in with your senses: Take in the scenery, look around, smell the air, listen to the sounds around you. How do you feel? The goal is to perceive something *new*. This trains your brain to see what actually is, rather than what your brain *perceives* to be true.

It's easy for our brains to get bogged down in the fear and stress of a massive report, those taxes you've been putting off, or that company project that feels too big to begin. Our brains naturally fall into patterned programs that tell us "there's not enough time" or "you're just going to fail, why even start?" This is when those alarms can really help address the deeper issue by shaking you conscious of your instinct and allowing you to break free of old, un-useful neural patterns. When you're feeling stressed, take time to address your survival instinct directly by asking: "*What am I afraid of in this moment? Am I allowing my fear to stop me before I even start?*" When you can look directly at the story you are telling yourself you might find that it's full of holes—ones that are meant to help you *survive* of course, but are currently preventing you from making the best decisions and attaining your goals. Simply by labeling the fear, you begin to take back control over it. It's not a tiger and it's not going to eat you. The new reality you paint can help you to dive in, fully prepared for success.

A break in pattern, even momentarily, allows you to stem the daily bombardment of stress and cortisol that's harming your mental and physical health. Instead, you begin to process your world like our hero from *The Matrix*. Suddenly what your brain was seeing as bullets careening toward you is in fact only a constant influx of emails, text messages, and news alerts. Your brain gets to reassess and re-record the threat for what it really is. You probably hadn't even registered the way those beeps and tones were stressing you out. But now? Now, you have new footage that consciously incorporates those sounds…and you dancing to them! The bullets fall from their original trajectories, harmless.

Timebending Hacks

- Try going through the entire day using your non-dominant hand (e.g., brushing your teeth, pouring your coffee, texting on your phone). All the little things that seem mindless will become novel again (especially true if you try to play sports!).
- Check in with your senses: Look around, smell the air, listen to the sounds, and try to perceive something new.
- Change the route you drive to work or to the grocery store—some little switch-up. Or if you use a navigation system, try turning it off and reaching your destination from memory. If you get a little lost, that's great! Along the way, you'll pay closer attention to geographical details you hadn't noticed when you weren't trying to actively create a mental map.

"Most people have the capacity to control the contents of their consciousness through simple mind management," says clinical psychologist and cognitive neuroscientist Ian Robertson. When you take the time to become more aware, consciously notice your surroundings, and label sensory inputs as *benign* or *exciting*. This helps your brain record new footage that slows your perception of time.

Notice I only mention labeling sensory inputs as benign or exciting. While surely there is a time for "scary" labels, as scientists continue to deepen our understanding of the emotion-related regions of the brain, we are

- Smile every time you see something orange.
- Eat your lunch in a new location, with new people, or try something you've never had (and would *never* typically order).
- Keep a list of positive things that happen throughout the day. They can be small—a stranger smiling at you on the street, or a dog greeting you with his whole body wiggling, the smell of the pavement after a rainfall. This can be a mental list, but for an even bigger benefit jot it down. Our brains are wired for negativity bias, so actively seeking out positive things for which we are grateful has been found in several scientific studies to have a range of benefits that extend even beyond slowing time.

finding that the relationship between cortisol and mood states is anything but straightforward. In fact, by injecting positive novelty into situations, you trick your brain into redirecting that surge of cortisol from anxiety and fear to useful excitement and motivation.

My sister used to say, "Life is either an ordeal or an adventure." In most of the situations in which we find ourselves, we can choose to direct our energy from a feeling of anxiety toward one of excitement.

Imagine the level of stress most of us would feel if we had to deliver a bad performance review. These conversations are often fraught with anxiety and concern. We let our ancient fears drive us, (*What if they reject me or kick me out of the tribe?*), wasting immeasurable amounts of time worrying about the outcome of how someone else will perceive the information. The reality is, we only get to control one story: our own. We can control our own stress by choosing excitement, making others more likely to respond with the same contagious positive outlook. And owing to the social nature of humans, emotions like anxiety and calm are both actually "contagious" in that they are mirrored in the brains of those we surround ourselves with. Rather than seeing the delivery of a bad performance review as an ordeal, think of it as an adventure. Feedback is truly a gift! How lucky we are to have an opportunity to empower others to grow! This is how you begin to master your survival instinct, which increases your ability to perform optimally. Win. Win.

It's far too easy for us to ignore or miss the conscious actions we need to take when we are wrapped up in the stress and busyness of the world around us, a world in which alarming levels of stress continue to grow. The irony is that, all things considered, we tend to live significantly less difficult, more secure lives than our forebears. We must lead our brains to the recognition that the environment we live in *now* requires a different kind of response than our ancestral environment did.

The antidote to relentless survival-mode stress may seem counterintuitive, but it's highly effective: Create a slowdown. Take the opportunity to control time rather than allowing time to control you. Stop fetching water with holes in your bucket. Take the time to find/see/acknowledge the holes and patch your pails. Notice the scurrying all around you and be different. Be novel. Listen to the music—whether it's a virtuoso violinist or beeping phone alerts. And assess danger with a fully conscious mind, so that your survival instinct doesn't steal time and rob you of the abundance all around you.

Chapter 1: Key Takeaways

- Your survival instinct is at the root of all other instincts.
- In the ancestral environment, our survival instinct kept us safe from life-threatening scenarios, but in a modern world it causes us undue stress on our brains, bodies, relationships, and work performance.
- Find ways to engage in *festina lente*: Make haste slowly to reduce stress and optimize productivity.
- Batch tasks to ensure time for deep work.
- Set awareness alarms for a conscious check-in.
- Seek novelty to bend time and experience life more slowly.
- Keep a gratitude journal to help overcome negativity bias.
- Use your conscious power to interpret the signal of stress as an adventure rather than an ordeal.

Sex

Redefining Roles, Leadership, and Responsibility

A S A TRADITION, MY FAMILY has always gathered for momentous occasions, and my great-grandmother's ninetieth birthday was no exception. It was at this event that I first began to fully recognize the powerful instinct that is our sex drive.

I was thirteen at the time, and I honestly don't remember much about the day. My sister and I were fighting for the attention of our younger cousins. There was probably some card-playing—a requisite for family gatherings. One moment, however, will be embedded in my mind permanently. We were gathering outside for a portrait. All the relatives—there had to be at least fifteen of us—smushed in close for the photo. My uncle set the shutter timer and ran back to join the pack, telling everyone to "say cheese." And then it happened.

"Cheese? Cheese?!" my great-grandmother offered in a tone of great offense. "I've lived for ninety years. I'll be damned if the best thing you can come up with to make us smile is cheese." And with a grin and a twinkle in her eye she said it...

"SEX!!!"

Needless to say, the photograph capturing the shock and horror on all of our faces has become a classic. A ninety-year-old, far past her reproductive prime, still had sex on the brain.

Birds do it. Bees do it. Barnacles, naked mole rats, and yes, you and I ~~you's and me's~~ (and apparently grannies too) do it. Sex is ubiquitous in the animal world and the second-most essential instinct after survival (after all, if you don't survive, well, you've eliminated the need for sex right there).

Getting a better sense of how our sex instinct has shaped the behaviors and motivations of both genders is essential to ensure a healthy professional and personal life. Our sex instinct basically shapes us in two distinct ways:

1. *Who we are attracted to, and why, drives us to conform to particular roles and stereotypes.* For the purposes of this book, I've stuck to heterosexual, cis, gender roles. It's not meant to marginalize

any portion of the population, but, rather, to inform the majority. Even if you fall outside of this population, the assumptions of gender and gender norms will still likely be applicable.

2. *Variation in sexual investment and motivation between the genders reinforces gender-typical roles.* Conversely, it can lead to negative consequences when miscommunication or misaligned goals result in sexual harassment.

What's *your* type when it comes to a mate? And why is that your preference? And what is the biggest behavior that leaves you open to sexual harassment suits (almost guaranteed not to be in your current organization's policy handbook)? You may think you know, but you'll likely be surprised at some of the profound ways your biology is undermining you with instinctive behaviors.

Biological Roles, Rules, and Ramifications

Ancestrally, women were valued for their ability to maintain cohesive, cooperative groups that helped to keep offspring safe, while the traditionally physically stronger and more dominant males were off hunting. This gender-specific selection still holds across most mammals. Females are valued for their ability to bear and raise children, while males are valued for status and the protection and resources that such status confers.

While we think we've moved past such antiquated norms, there's a reason why women in the United States spend upward of $450 billion annually on beauty products. For 200,000-plus years, the best way for females to get access to resources was through a high-status male. To date, we are *still* trying to look young and "symmetrical"—a proxy for reproductive viability and health—to draw the attention of the best men. Because male instinctual predilection still drives many men's mate selection, women do all manner of strange things to appeal to potential mates. Injecting toxins into our faces (botox), or using waist trainers and corsets that are more like torture devices are just two examples. And there seems to be a prevailing phenomenon that the older women get the lighter they dye their hair. Well, there may be something to that old adage that "gentlemen prefer blondes." No woman over reproductive age is "naturally" blond— our hair inherently darkens or grays as we age, so gentlemen who prefer blondes may be responding to blond hair as a reference point of youthfulness and, therefore, mate-value.

It's also no coincidence that the waist-to-hip ratio of *Playboy* centerfolds and Miss America winners has been amazingly consistent since the 1920s. What's so magical about a waist-to-hip ratio of 0.7? It's a proportion that allows maximal fertility. We find that ratio aesthetically pleasing only in that in confers a benefit for reproduction. Even though we live in a time when we can actively avoid pregnancy by using contraception, our minds still draw us toward individuals who would bear our children most effectively.

Males, too, have their own peculiar ways to signify status and gain access to mates. You have probably seen a peacock's beautiful tail plumes (meant to impress the peahens) or an intimidating rack of antlers on a buck (which demonstrates virility and can be used to intimidate rivals). Similarly, human men rely on "positional consumption" to demonstrate their mate-value and remind rivals that they are "the best." Men spend enough money on luxury brands like Ferrari, Lamborghini, and Rolex that luxury advertisers overwhelmingly target men. Amazingly, in studies in which researchers artificially elevate the male sex hormone testosterone (to the higher levels it naturally would reach around attractive females), men select high-status, name-brand versions of watches and apparel over a selection of higher *quality* versions. They are actively trying to demonstrate their status without the benefit of a peacock's tail or a buck's antler rack.

It's the same reason that men are often concerned with their height, and why politicians are adding lifts to their shoes and standing on platforms behind podiums. Why the need to appear taller? Because women prefer taller men (and apparently so do other men when they are voting these men into positions of power). Taller men would have achieved higher status in the challenging environments of our ancestors. Height once allowed men to be more dominant hunters, warriors, and protectors of resources. Today, we see this preference play out in bizarre ways. For example, among the general population of American males, those over six feet tall represent a measly 14.5 percent. But when you narrow that population to include only male CEOs of Fortune 500 companies, the percentage of men over six feet tall leaps to 58 percent! A 2013 study analyzing American presidential height concluded that the last president who was shorter than the average American was William McKinley, elected in 1896! The researchers estimated that candidate height can account for as much as 15 percent of the outcome in elections. The sex instinct that equates height with status is likely the driving force that often puts tall men in positions of power. The logical preferences of our ancestors are still showing up today as behavioral ghosts, from politics to boardrooms, without any logical association between height and leadership ability.

Our cultural reinforcement of gender-value norms even applies to the concerns we have for our offspring. The aggregated data from millions of people across the globe conducting Google searches demonstrate that the likely words to follow "is my son..." are "genius" or "gifted," whereas the similar search "is my daughter..." was most commonly finished with the words "ugly" or "overweight." This is troubling. When it comes to gender, we are still wrestling with the importance of appearance for women and status for men as indicators of worth. And the problems don't stop there.

Sex Strategies

Sex instincts shape our behavior in ways that can ultimately cause miscommunication and misaligned goals
between the genders if we aren't consciously directing
(and redirecting) those behaviors. This is because men
and women aren't just relying on different signals to demonstrate and determine mate value, but also approach
reproduction with two completely different strategies.

Before we get to the trouble with sex, put on your biologist lens for a moment and consider the ways in which
old-fashioned reproduction is significantly more energetically expensive for females. Think about how much
more work a female must invest in the production of an
egg, its gestation, avoiding the dangers of childbirth, the
nursing of offspring, and so forth. Having a child is an extraordinarily energetically expensive endeavor, and
females have a limited number of opportunities to produce viable offspring. Women are only reproductively
viable for a short period of time (from puberty until
menopause). Compare this to their male counterparts,
whose sperm is typically viable up until death at any age!
As a result, women tend to be more discriminating about
their choice of a mate. Think about our ancestral mothers: Carrying a fetus to term at nine months, then being
its only source of food and energy in the form of nutrient-
and fat-rich breast milk for several years, is no easy feat.
What's more is that during that time, females were at
their most vulnerable as their abilities to forage and

escape predators were significantly reduced. As such, there was strong pressure for females to choose a *high-quality* mate (furthering the male drive for status)— someone with good genetics, who was a good provider and protector.

Males, on the other hand, are in another reproductive game entirely. For men, the mating game is about seeking out young, symmetrical women—and lots of them! Not man-bashing here, it's just how male brains are wired. Sperm is cheap to make (~500 million per ejaculation). *Biologically* there is nothing required of a man for the development of his offspring from ejaculation forward. As a result, males don't have to be as cognizant of mate *quality* (Who cares if she can't raise the offspring super successfully if you have one hundred other opportunities this month?). When it comes to sex, the instinct for men is to seek *quantity*—particularly with reproductively fit women (driving the selection for idealized notions of beauty).

The biological differences in the costs of reproduction and in our mate-attracting strategies mean that male and female brains are wired to think and operate differently. The ripple effects of our instinct for sex, and how we engage in seeking mates, have far-reaching implications in our personal and professional worlds.

For 200,000 years, males have been selected for their status, dominance, and ability to provide resources. So what happened in the course of the last one hundred years as females have begun to move into the traditional space of men? When the ability to survive and garner resources independent of men became more accessible, women exploded into the spaces that had traditionally been reserved for males (including the workplace). What's played out in headquarters around the world has been a dramatic behavioral science experiment on a massive scale.

Modern Misalignments

It should come as no surprise that there are significant inter-gender conflicts as women become more and more prevalent and powerful in the workplace, taking on high-status jobs that men traditionally occupied. Men aren't just feeling a cultural displacement, but likely also a conscious or subconscious visceral, envious, and threatened response to women who have (at least according to their sex instinct) knocked them out of contention of being a more attractive mate. In fact, this is exactly what research demonstrates. A study published in *Personnel Psychology* found that the same qualities that help an applicant of either gender attain a job subsequently hurt the performance evaluations of the women candidates. In other words, a woman has to be competent to be hired, but that same high competency will result in lower performance evaluations, in particular from men in positions of high dominance. Visibility as a high-achieving female is punished.

Another team of researchers at Washington State University found that men's behavioral reactions to women in positions of power went far beyond poor ratings. In negotiation exercises, male subordinates were more assertive when paired with a female of higher status. In one scenario, men were asked to negotiate the split of a $10,000 bonus with a female manager. The biggest factor that determined how evenly he made the split of the bonus was whether or not the female supervisor was described as "power seeking or ambitious" (in which case he offered significantly less of the share relative to when the female manager was not described in ambitious or power-seeking terms). The researchers followed this scenario by immediately administering an implicit threat test—a test widely used in social science research to uncover subconscious associations. The men were asked to identify words that appeared on a computer screen for a fraction of a second. Those who'd negotiated with female bosses described as "ambitious" were more likely to see words like "fear," "risk," and "threat," indicating that they did in fact, at least subconsciously, feel threatened by these "power-seeking" women even if they didn't *consciously* admit it.

But men aren't the only ones fighting biological battles at work. Females in the workplace often struggle to be taken seriously, especially when they become parents. Despite evidence from a 2011 Zenger Folkman survey of 7,280 leaders demonstrating that females rank higher than their male counterparts in fifteen of the sixteen competencies that top leaders exemplify most (as rated by their employees), females are ranked as less competent and less committed to work as soon as their status as a mother is revealed. Men do not experience a drop in competency ratings when they are dually labeled as a father. In fact, male leaders who are also fathers are perceived as more responsible! Our instincts are once again interfering with our better judgment. As soon as we are reminded that women, even powerful, responsible, qualified leaders, are mothers, our sex instinct fires up ancient associations that hold women back. But the flip side of gender bias must also be given due consideration.

A Harvard and U.S. Naval Academy study as well as a Pew Research Center survey have confirmed a phenomenon known as the "Women are Wonderful" effect (or WAW for short). This is the sociological tendency to assign and rate women higher on traits around compassion and empathy, a likely associative nod toward the nurturing evolutionary roots of women. But as a 2019 article in *Bloomberg Businessweek* so clearly articulates, plunking women into leadership positions because of our positive associations with a gender is no guarantee of an ethical, respectful, or well-run workplace: "Suggesting women are innately different than men is the kind of gender essentialism that results in fewer women at the top in the first place."

It's not about which gender is "better" in leadership roles. The reality is we need the traditional skill sets of both males and females. Leadership is a genderless domain, but recognizing how our instincts have shaped both men *and* women to feel threatened by a woman who is "taking our status" or by a stay-at-home dad who "isn't a valuable resource contributor" is essential in intervening when our instincts might lead us down a dangerous path.

In 2018, I conducted a series of experiments in which I asked high-powered executive women to participate in a version of an Implicit Association Test (IAT). Implicit Association Tests measure the minuscule time differences that your brain takes to associate two concepts. For example, you'd be able to more quickly respond to the word "beach" having been primed with "sand" or "sun" rather than an unrelated word like "paper clip." The reason for this is that your brain has been wired to connect these concepts through either evolutionary or cultural programming. Last time you were at the beach you probably experienced sand, so there are a greater number of connections in your brain associating sand and beach than paper clip and beach. The end result is that you're faster at pairing sand/beach and slower at pairing paper clip/beach. This concept can be used to access your subconscious and test less innocuous pairings. In this case, I asked the female CEOs to work with words that were associated with "family" (parent, child, sibling) and words that were associated with "leaders" (boss, CEO, power) and pair these words with either male or female faces.

The results shocked me. A full 95 percent of these powerful female leaders were faster to associate "leader" words with male faces and "family" words with female faces. How could powerful women, leaders in their own right, not quickly recognize their image in a female face and associate it with leadership qualities?

The answer is that our sex instinct has deeply sculpted our perceptions of gender in ways that logically no longer apply today.

I was still reeling from the results of the IAT study when I picked up a business book in my local airport and was forced to confront my own bias. The title had caught my eye, but then I was immediately turned off when I noticed the name on the cover belonged to a woman. It was a painful recognition. As a successful businesswoman who was speaking and writing about these exact biases, my instinctive reaction was still to find less value in a business book authored by another female. As I was writing this very book, I gave serious pause to whether or not I wanted to include my full author name, or leave it as R. Heiss to avoid these uncomfortable but very real biases. It seems you, my smart reader, have already overridden any instinctual hesitation you might have had in purchasing a business book authored by a woman, but science has found these instincts are not often so readily overcome.

Studies featuring identical résumés with a single significant difference—the name at the top—begin to clue us in to this phenomenon. Numerous researchers have found that even when candidates have the same qualifications, a male name on the résumé led recruiters to perceive the candidate as more qualified, competent, and worthy of a significantly higher compensation offer than résumé candidates with female names.

Why aren't we giving women a fair shot in the work-force? Let's look again back to the qualities for which men and women have been selected for hundreds of thousands of years.

In June 2018, Ernst & Young, one of the largest accounting firms in the world, landed itself in hot water when it offered promising up-and-coming female leaders a training called, "Power-Presence-Purpose." The training included tips like the following:

- Clothing must flatter, but short skirts are a no-no.
- Women should look healthy and fit, with a "good haircut" and "manicured nails."
- Don't directly confront men in a meeting; it's perceived as aggressive.
- Don't talk to a man face-to-face. Cross your legs and sit at an angle to him.

In 2017, a year before Ernst & Young offered this erstwhile training guide, Google fired software engineer James Damore whose internal memo, dubbed "Google's Ideological Echo Chamber," sparked outrage internally and in discussion groups across the country. In the memo Damore reasoned that, based on the brain patterning of males and females, Google shouldn't be spending so much money trying to recruit females into their engineering space, implying that males were more suited for such work.

On the surface, both the Ernst & Young training and the leaked Google memo seem beyond cringe worthy.

But it's worth taking a step back to appreciate the under-lying biology that lays the groundwork for both of these perspectives. Of course, the "Power-Presence-Purpose" training is deeply offensive. And *of course* women should be recruited as engineers, right? Then again, the *ultimate* reasoning for such cringe-worthy arguments might just be sound.

Reader, before you revolt, hear me out.

WOMEN: I'm not arguing that you need to accom-modate men and bend over backward to protect their fragile egos.

MEN: I'm not suggesting that you are all so delicate that you can't handle a challenge from a well-qualified woman.

That said, when we understand how sexual selection has shaped our instincts, the training that suggests how I, as a woman, should dress to be taken seriously, or how I should approach a man in a workplace setting in a manner that doesn't challenge his status in front of others, actually, sort of, makes sense (at least from the an-cestral context).

In an ideal world, we would all be enlightened be-ings operating from our conscious, higher-level brains. And as such, we wouldn't need such absurd, backward-sounding advice. No woman should have to tiptoe around a man's status as a way to advance or even ensure the safety of her own career. But I'd also argue that no man should be fired for challenging hiring incentives aimed to recruit females. Damore's argument wasn't that females *couldn't* do the work, but rather that (on average) women weren't as naturally inclined to the systems work Google engineers were being asked to do. My emphasis would be placed on the *on average* across a normally distributed population bit of his argument. Not that individual women weren't equally as capable or *more* capable than any number of men, but *on average* within a population, this argument holds.

At the time of this writing, women still make up a small percentage (~17.8 percent) of Google's technical staff in spite of well over $100 million a year being poured into diversity initiatives. Damore's point was that perhaps Google was throwing money at a problem that didn't need fixing. Perhaps this is just the natural state of differences between male and female brains.

Without a doubt, our biological pulls are not experienced in a vacuum. Socialization and cultural gendered norms are informed by, and then reinforced by, our biological nature. One striking example is a study that found that when women are reminded of stereotypes associated with their sex (e.g., women aren't as good at math as men are), their performance on a subsequent math test suffers. These stereotypes repeated consciously (or not) by teachers, parents, and peers certainly play into deepening the biological norms that exist and worsening any natural talent that exists outside of those norms. But what I find most striking is how we have "corrected for"

some of these socialization practices by exposing and encouraging more young women in STEM (science,
technology, engineering, mathematics) careers, but
haven't been doing the same thing for young men, by exposing and encouraging them in the home and early
childhood education fields.

While I don't mean to undermine the very real problem of bias in hiring (see above: women get the short end
of the stick even when they present identical skill sets), or
in recruitment, training, advancement, pay, and a plethora of other issues that women are shorted on in the
workplace, we often overlook one of the biggest sources
of these biases. It's not that there aren't enough females
being recruited to be engineers. It's that societally, we
value engineers more than we value, say, elementary
school teachers. At least when it comes to status and pay.
Hence glorifying our efforts to encourage young women
to pursue traditionally male-based industries, but not re-
ciprocating when it comes to encouraging our young men
in the fields that are traditionally reserved for women.

The monetary and status-derived value we put on traditional "women's work" is significantly lower than the
traditionally male-dominated positions. Damore made a
point that Google shouldn't be spending millions of dollars to recruit females to engineering positions. Perhaps
instead, there's an argument to be made that we *should* be
spending that kind of money to recruit males to elementary school teaching positions. After all, the percentage of
male elementary school teachers, 11 percent, is lower than

the female technical staff at Google, 17.8 percent. While a few modest initiatives do attempt to recruit men into these jobs, we certainly don't see millions of dollars being poured into diversity initiatives in elementary schools. Jobs in education have been vastly devalued because they are traditionally aligned with females.

As genders go, males and females are not equal. We never have been. As a collective whole, our biology has uniquely shaped us to excel in particular arenas and re-quire support in others. To be clear: That does not mean there isn't individual variation.

Unfortunately, our minds don't care much for individ-ual cases that break gender norms, such as women who might make exceptional programmers at Google, or men who are the very best early-education specialists (let alone those individuals who identify as nonbinary). Our brains are wired to group people into categories and label them with group identities (something we will explore in Chapter 5). Because we live in an environment of 8 billion people, our brains make shortcuts that allow us to categorize, on average, the greatest number of people. Unfortunately, that means, sometimes, we get it wrong. Are there females who are naturally better engineers and coders than any male? Absolutely. Are there males who are naturally better caregivers than any female? Without a doubt. But our current methods of hiring and promot-ing are likely short-circuited in our brains and we miss these exceptions to the "norm." We don't recognize "Dar-rel, the incredible caretaker" as Darrel. We see him as a man and quickly categorize him with the usual associated traits. Kim isn't "Kim the engineer," she's a woman who is categorized along the normal curve with all the other women. But even if the Kims and the Darrels of the world only make up a measly 1 percent of the global population, that means we are mis-categorizing 160 million people with instinctive gendered norms that don't align with their actual skill sets.

While Damore's argument may have had *some* biological merit, the finer points of it warranted significant further discussion. Unfortunately, Google's reactionary reflex to Damore's statement was to immediately terminate his employment. To me, this is the scariest reaction for a company to take.

When employees are willing to engage in challenging conversations, it is a *huge* game changer, and no one should be punished or penalized if we can *assume positive intent* and have a bigger discussion around the topic. We have to stop being afraid of engaging in topics that seem politically charged or motivated, and instead allow science to guide our discussions. People come to work as *humans*, with their own instincts, beliefs, and ideas. The more we can engage with one another as *individuals*, rather than as genders or races or some other marker that our brains wish to use for simple categorization purposes, the more likely we will be to judge a person for their *actual* skills and abilities. But it takes a willingness to wrestle with the contradictions and complications of our categorizing instincts—and with the individuals who break norms.

For some of the same reasons, it took me a long time to find my voice in the world of diversity in business because I was so afraid of saying the wrong thing. (*What's the appropriate title: Black, African American, people of color? How do I reference the gender nonconforming community?*) Instead of defending or championing a position, I stayed silent, like so many others. Today, I live by a mantra borrowed from renowned social scientist Brené Brown: *I'm not here to be right, I'm here to get it right.* Science isn't politically affiliated. I'm here to follow science and speak from it. Silence due to fear of punishment is arguably the most restrictive, isolating move a person (or organization) can employ, and yet, it is one of the go-to strategies for anyone who feels disempowered. In extreme cases of fear, gender plays another outsize role when silence isn't so much a choice as it is a survival strategy.

Sexual Harassment—Grinning and Bearing It

I was old enough to know better. I'm not even sure what that means or at what age there's a point when suddenly you "know better." But for whomever is keeping track of that magically appropriate age—I was past it.

I was a professional. A strong, athletic, five-foot-ten woman with a PhD and little fear of any person. Or, at least, no fear of which I was aware of as I sat in a restaurant on a hot Southern summer day.

My phone rang. It was my friend letting me know he was stuck in traffic and would be about forty-five minutes late. Bummer. But there are far worse things in life than having to sit with a laptop, eating chips and salsa. And for the moment, things seemed to have gotten even better: A beer arrived at my table, compliments of a man from across the room. I'm not a huge drinker, especially not at lunch, but I figured, "What the heck?"

I didn't want to seem rude, so I graciously accepted the drink and waved my thanks at the gentleman who had sent it my way. That's where this story should end. And I wish that it did.

I sat sipping my beer and working on my laptop, oblivious to the fact that someone had slipped in the booth beside me. I was startled when I looked up to find myself physically trapped by the man who had sent me a beer. I didn't feel threatened, just surprised.

I smiled and thanked him again, but quickly turned back to my work to signal that I wasn't interested in any further conversation. But he leaned in closer and started talking to me. I answered in short grunts of acknowledgment, feigning the least amount of interest I could, while walking the thin line of rudeness. I didn't want to be impolite. Yet his chatter persisted and then his hand found its way to my leg.

Now I was annoyed.

"I'm sorry, I'm really busy here. I appreciate the drink but I need to work." That should have been clear enough.

Wrong again. He moved in closer, pinning me against the wall of my booth.

Let me pause here to indicate that I wasn't actually feeling a physical threat. I'm a tall, athletic woman and could push my way past this man and put him on the floor if I so chose. But about now is when I started to hear *the voice*. And it's a voice that too many women know well. It's a voice that tells us: *Be nice. Don't make a scene. This guy was just trying to buy you a drink. Don't hurt his pride.*

Meanwhile, his hand had found its way back to my knee and was quickly moving up. I felt the stickiness of the vinyl booth beneath my right thigh as I tried to slide farther away. A hundred soda mishaps and salsa spills pulling at my skin.

"No. Please. No. I have a friend who will be here any minute. I need to work. Please go back to your table."

His hand was on my waist now. My eyes darted around the room, trying to find someone who could help me out of the situation gracefully. Every pair of eyes I met flashed a knowing look of sympathy, then they quickly went back to their respective plates. No one wanted to interfere in the situation any more than I wanted to make a scene.

I removed his hand from my body for the fifth or sixth time, resigned to the fact that he was not going to give up. Inside, I wanted to scream and kick and punch and yell into his imprudent face: *What gives you the right?! I've made it obvious that your advances are not welcome. Now go away!* But every time my voice escaped my lips it was in an apologetic whisper: "I'm sorry, you don't seem to understand. Please stop touching me."

I didn't want to be *that* girl. That helpless female who causes a scene and embarrasses a man who was "only trying to be kind." Believe me when I say that I know I had every right to.

My friend finally came bursting through the door. I had been texting him about the entire situation. Despite my friend's text encouragements to just leave, I had sat, pinned in my booth, removing the unwanted hands of this stranger for forty-five minutes. That is not an exaggeration: *forty-five minutes.*

Fortunately, my friend made quick work of the situation, physically lifting the man from his seat after he didn't seem to understand the initial polite request that he should move. No violence ensued. No big ruckus. Just me flushing wildly and cursing myself for having to be rescued. What the hell had happened? My friend hadn't done anything that I wasn't capable of doing myself. So why hadn't I acted?

I've since replayed the situation in my head, with me as an onlooker. I know that, as a bystander, I would've had no problem removing the man the way my friend had and playing the "hero" for the woman pinned in the booth. But instead, I acted in direct conflict with my strongly held beliefs. By that I mean, I had previously never believed the voices that said: *A woman should never hurt a man's pride,* or *A woman shouldn't cause a scene.*

But apparently, this only held true when that woman was *anyone* but me. I had outwardly rejected those schemas, but the truths around which my brain was structured created a huge paradox.

This man had *zero* impact on my life outside of that moment. He was not my boss. Not my colleague. Not even anyone I'd ever likely run into again, and yet I *still* couldn't find a way to assert myself. Imagine how much more difficult the entire situation would have been had any of those conditions been true—if he'd been my boss, my adviser, my co-worker.

Unwanted sexual contact, particularly from males, is not an uncommon phenomenon in the natural world. But it is, of course, highly unacceptable in the world in which we now live. As the #MeToo and #TimesUp campaigns have brought more exposure to the frequency of sexual harassment in the workplace, we face the nauseating reminder that we, as humans, are still struggling to manage our sex instincts properly. Beyond the very real human dignity costs, it's also costing companies huge monetary sums.

While the latest figures on the cost of sexual harassment are woefully out of date, estimates in federal government workplaces from the early 1990s put the figure at $327 million over a two-year period. Unfortunately, despite all the work and attention paid to movements like #MeToo and #TimesUp, the data on sexual harassment haven't budged. In fact, between 2015 and 2019 the Equal Employment Opportunity Commission actually saw an annual increase of 10.1 percent in sexual harassment charges.

Add up the emotional and sometimes physical costs of harassment, the massive legal fees, the substantial research demonstrating reduced employee motivation, increased turnover, and decreased productivity, the ripple effects across the entire culture of an office and the final tab for our misguided sex instincts are much too high to ignore.

This is where a clear understanding and appreciation for the variation in sexual investment between genders become particularly relevant.

Research has found that the male brain is primed for sexual over-perception. This means, essentially, that men think women are into them a lot more than they actually are. A 2003 study published in the *Journal of Research in Personality* found that when a woman smiles or touches a man's arm, men are more likely to misinterpret these cues as an invitation for sexual advances. That's just the sex instinct at work, ensuring that men don't miss an opportunity to mate. After all, evolutionarily, it's far more costly for a man to miss an opportunity to produce offspring with a willing woman than it is for him to pursue a woman who isn't necessarily interested. Subconscious or not, this over-perception tendency often leads to miscommunication—particularly when one considers the female perspective.

Reproductive investment is significantly more biologically expensive for females (nine months is a long time!), so women tend to be more cautious about the selection of their mates.

So let's break this down. When a man demonstrating sexual interest approaches a woman, what are her best options as a modern woman if she is not interested? Here's how her instinct may unconsciously assess the situation:

1. **SHOULD SHE REJECT HIM?** A 2018 study on "Predicting men's immediate reactions to a simulated date's sexual rejection" suggests this wouldn't be such a great idea. Aggression and violence are common responses to sexual rejection. "Men have been taught since the earliest of times to protect their masculinity," notes psychotherapist Jaime Gleicher. "When they're rejected, they associate it with their masculinity. When that's threatened by an outside source, they tend to fight for it—also as a way to re-prove their manliness." The rejection of a drink might, to a man, feel more like the stripping of his very masculinity. Perhaps there is a better alternative.

2. **SHOULD SHE RUN AWAY?** Or fight him off? In a stressful situation, our fight-or-flight option should kick in. But likely neither of these responses will be favorable as men tend to be faster and physically more dominant.

3. **SHOULD SHE FREEZE, SMILE, AND APPEASE?** This is often the choice our instincts make for us.

Why? Perhaps because a smile is the natural, nearly universal response indicating social discomfort. When you aren't sure how to respond, a smile seems a good bet. It's an indicator of submission and goodwill. But the *dominance-status hypothesis* gives us a slightly darker interpretation of this flash of teeth.

The reason the female brain cues a smile when feeling threatened, according to this well-supported hypothesis, has more to do with power dynamics. Women smile to show compliance as the socially and physically weaker sex in order to mediate the situation—often leading us right back to male-brain miscues and misinterpretations. She may not even be consciously aware that she's smiling, any more than he's consciously aware of misreading her nervous smile as interest.

In a revealing 2001 study, psychologists interviewed 197 women about how they might react to inappropriate professional job interview questions, like "Do you wear a bra to work?" and "Do you feel that you're sexually desirable?" While each woman responded that they wouldn't stand for such behavior, their actions spoke otherwise. When a selection of these women were later faced with similar questions in what they believed to be a real job interview, each answered the questions and stayed for the duration of what must have been an excruciatingly uncomfortable process. In follow-up interviews, each woman said she had felt fear during the job interview, which translated into smiles plastered on their faces like beacons of non-threatening pleas.

Awareness to Action: Ushering In an Era of Responsibility That Transcends the Sex Instinct

We deserve to override our sex instincts and appreciate the offerings of each gender without the fear of losing our status as valuable contributors. The misalignment of our reproductive interests should never land us in situations where we are the unwilling victim or the perpetrator of sexual harassment.

So how can we begin to intervene in instincts so deeply embedded in each of us? I think the key here is to first develop a real *awareness* of how each of our genders behaves in a heightened state. Researcher George Loewenstein refers to different physiological states as "hot" or "cold." A cold state is one in which a person is logical, and not emotionally heightened. In the example above, it would refer to the women who were originally asked how they would behave if they were sitting in a job interview where they were asked highly inappropriate questions. Because those women are only *imagining* that situation, they remain in a cold state. Loewenstein argues there is an understanding gap between our hot and cold selves that we have difficulty reconciling. In a hot state we can't imagine how we would behave differently than how we already are, and the same holds true for when we are in a cold state. When I was feeling trapped in that restaurant booth, for example, I couldn't imagine punching my way out. But sitting here today, I can't imagine me *not*. It's as if we are two separate people entirely without access to understanding how intense feelings will overwhelm us in any particular circumstance.

In fact, when Loewenstein's team tested the behaviors of males in an experimental setting, he found that men who were sexually aroused (a "hot" state) were more likely to encourage a woman to drink to excess (to lower her resistance to sex), more willing to drug her drink, and more likely to continue to push her for sex after she expressly said "no." The same men, when tested in a non-sexually aroused, or "cold" state, were more respectful of women's boundaries.

When we begin to see how men and women in two hot states (sexual arousal and fear, respectively) abandon their cold-state logic, it becomes plain how a dangerous situation could unfold. This may seem like the dramatic end of the scale, but scary scenarios often evolve from insignificant origins. Consider how easy it might be for you or your colleagues to roll your eyes during any sexual harassment training. Of course it seems absurd that you would ever put yourself in any such compromising circumstance—but then again, remember how little our cold-state self understands or relates to our hot-state behaviors. Opening the discussion around sexual harassment at work by prominently featuring information about hot and cold states could dramatically change the seriousness with which people approach these important trainings.

Heightened awareness around our sex instinct goes beyond harassment. We all must be active sentinels in the ways in which we define and give value to traditional gender roles as well. I recently asked a mixed-gender group of CEOs to conduct a thought experiment with me. I'd purchased a dozen magazines and scattered them around the tables so everyone had access. The goal of the exercise was to adopt the identity of an extraterrestrial who was studying these magazines to get a sense of both genders: What defined a female or male according to our culture? I supplemented this task by asking everyone in the group to name the top five leadership books or podcasts that they most recently consumed. The conclusions we reached were painstakingly clear:

1. Women are creatures meant to be beautiful, slim, and young. Advertising targeting women was specifically around creams, makeup, and parenting.
2. Men are creatures of status, size, and wealth. Advertising targeting men was specifically around bulking up, luxury products, and career advancement.
3. All of the leadership podcasts, social media influencers, and books read had been produced and/or written by men.

I want to be clear that I'm not admonishing men who are producing great content. We need male voices in leadership. They simply can't be the *only* voices. Even when I tried to broaden my research by asking Google to provide lists of the top leadership books, it returned lists that were 90 percent to 100 percent male authors. We have to be willing to look beyond the blinders of a single perspective of leadership. If we are going to intervene in the sex instinct, we need to give our brains alternative information.

What does this look like in practice? You can intentionally seek out information from people who provide content outside of your instinctually built perspectives. Open the framework for building new connections in your brain. For example, find a female podcaster who talks about leadership, or a male author who's written a book on housekeeping or parenting or grooming.

Force your instinctual brain to form new associations and new perspectives. Make a game of it. Ask friends, children, spouses, colleagues to try to catch you using gendered language (e.g., Would you use the term "girl boss"? How about "boy boss"? "Forewoman"? "Mr. Mom"?). It doesn't mean you have to walk around on eggshells, but it might help you to recognize associations and stereotypes you may unintentionally be holding toward one gender or another. You can even challenge yourself to start recognizing these associations by others.

One easy way to catch yourself is to do an instinct intervention game: Rerun in your mind an interaction you recently had with someone, but substitute the other party with a man, woman, child, or relative. If you wouldn't change anything about what you said or how you said it, you were likely safe from reinforcing a gendered norm. You can also flip it to think about how other people interact with you. Here's a simple example: I was recently asked to speak to a group made up primarily of men, and I had three separate interactions beforehand that I categorized as part of my instinct intervention game.

1. After shaking my hand, a man commented, "Wow, that's a great grip you've got there!" I wondered to myself if he would have said that had I been a man.

2. I stood up from talking with another man and his reaction was: "Quite the legs you've got there! Didn't realize when you were sitting that you were quite so tall." This was both a potential sexual advance and a threat to his status with my height. I gave myself two points for catching that.

3. As I was presenting a study directly from peer-reviewed scientific literature, a third man interrupted me to say, "I see the point you're trying to make there, sweetheart, but..." The very nature of his interruption undermines my authority in this subject, and then the addition of "sweetheart" takes it over the top.

I don't see any of these interjections as major infrac-
tions, but the everyday language we use and the
associations we make as a result become a cycle of reinforcement. Our brains are wired to repeat. The more
often we see and hear messages, the more likely we are
to be influenced by them. When we are dealing with the
power of an instinct like sex, that influence can easily reinforce negative behavioral patterns.

Take, for example, a stereotype with which we are
probably all familiar: blondes. Let's play a little game. I
want you to think about some of the words you associate
with the stereotypical blonde. Go ahead and jot them
down if you'd like, but don't cheat—just write the first
things that come to mind. I'm not going to judge you. I
don't think you are stereotyped against blondes just because you know the stereotype.

I'm guessing you may have come up with words like
"ditzy" and "dumb."

Now consider the names of a few celebrities or per-
sonalities that fit into the blonde stereotype.

When I do this exercise with groups to whom I'm
speaking, I almost always get the same answers. Goldie
Hawn, Pamela Anderson, Barbie. Care to guess the name
of a blonde that I've *never* gotten? In the thousands of
people that I have asked this question to, not a single one
responded with Ken doll. Or Brad Pitt. Or *any* male, for
that matter. I don't think you are biased against blondes,
but based on the responses I've gotten from thousands

of participants over the years, I'm beginning to suspect we *are* biased against women.

Think back to just a moment ago when you wrote down those negative words associated with the blonde stereotype, but recognize now that you would also naturally then have to associate those same words with the female gender. Dumb, ditzy, flighty—those only seem to apply to blondes if they are also female. Don't beat yourself up. You're not alone. I have yet to come across one person (of any gender) who gave the name of a blond male—independent of the respondent's gender. And that same stereotype works in the opposite direction as well when you change "blonde" to "jock." The trick is to start becoming aware of these subconscious associations so that we can begin to challenge them.

For example, women who brag about their accomplishments at work are rated more negatively and perceived as less competent on job-related tasks than men who boast about their achievements. This is an association we should be looking for and questioning our responses to. When Kelly talks about how smoothly her last call with that important client went, are we rolling our eyes or congratulating her the way we might Ted?

When it comes to the world of business, women find themselves constantly in a bind. Here are some common binds I hear from the women I consult with:

• You can be liked, but you'll be seen as incompetent.

- You can be competent, but you'll be viewed as a bitch.
- You can be feminine and not be seen as a leader.
- You can be masculine and be seen as arrogant or uppity.
- You can be aggressive and bossy.
- You can be passive and irrelevant.
- You can be a bad mom or a bad worker.
- You can be sweet or shrill.
- You can be a man-hating feminist or female betrayer.
- You can be pretty or smart.

The list goes on.

The perils for women who fail to pitch perfectly into that very narrow strike zone follow them even into the world of social media. In 2019, a study out of Cornell University found that female influencers on Instagram endured disparagement and harassment for being too honest (sharing private feelings or posting makeup-free photos, for example) *and* for being too fake (editing photos to perfection or never showing a messy house). One more bind to add to the list.

Men who break gender stereotypes by not being the primary breadwinners don't have it any easier. Stay-at-home dads in particular have become the butt of every joke in our television programs and movies. A 2013 study found that men who were not the primary earners in their households were more likely to seek treatment for anxiety, insomnia, and erectile dysfunction. Another study found these same men to be more likely to engage in extramarital affairs, a move the researchers suspected was an instinctual ploy to counter their compromised "manhood."

It might be easy to become bitter as you recognize the stories and associations that are being repeated about your gender, but we have the power to use this knowledge for good. Being aware of the ways in which our sex instinct influences us means we are then capable of stepping into a new era of *responsibility*. In a modern environment in which we are not under the daily threat of survival, it is imperative that we take on active roles to challenge our sex instinct and step in when we see it influencing the behavior of others, or ourselves, in inappropriate ways.

Sometimes this means literally stepping in, as a bystander might, to interfere when witnessing sexual harassment or negative gender-conforming language. We have all been there: Listening to Janet tell that cringeworthy sexist joke and being caught without a response; seeing a man in a restaurant getting too handsy with a stranger. Most of us don't want to address the problem directly, but there are a number of strategies that can be employed to combat the negative effects of our sex instincts. While direct confrontation of an offender will ultimately need to happen, the immediate context might not be the time in which to directly confront. Each strategy below involves immediately disrupting the infraction to keep everyone safe. Then, the appropriate person can address the offender in an appropriate setting.

1. **USE HUMOR.** Psychology professor Julie Woodzicka suggests that you can train your brain (and signal to others) that you disapprove of another's language and behaviors by having a few one-liners in your back pocket. For example: *Can you repeat yourself? I'm having a hard time hearing you over my eyes rolling.* This kind of response makes obvious to the offender that his or her behavior is disapproved of, without an explicit call out. Nevertheless, I'd caution that this strategy might be limited in its effectiveness, as sarcastic responses and fighting fire with fire are likely only effective across a similar power structure (colleague to colleague rather than boss to subordinate) and might fuel tensions.

2. **ABRUPTLY CHANGE THE SUBJECT.** Using Woodzicka's strategy, have a few nonsequitur topic changes at the ready. *What did you think of the game last night?* or *Have you ever noticed how many red trucks are driving around these days?* It doesn't have to be logical. In fact, it might be more effective if it's not. This breaks the pattern and forces everyone to step back into a "cooler" state again.

3. **EXCUSE YOURSELF AND THE TARGET.** Rather than directly confronting or interrupting the offender's assault, turn your attention to the victim. *Excuse me, Dan, I need to see you in the conference room for a quick minute. Can I steal you now?*

Our responsibility to intervene in our, or another's, sex instincts doesn't end with harassment. It carries over in the stories we tell about gender norms. As females, we can't continue the story that we are one another's competition. While this may not be a story any of us consciously tells, it shows up frequently in our hiring practices. One recent study found that women are 30 percent less likely to hire another attractive female. One reason may be that women are hardwired to compete for males' attention by using their looks (i.e., showing off their reproductive value in exchange for a male's protection/resources). I've never heard a director of HR sit across from a candidate and say, "Well, Cheryl, you are highly qualified for this position, and I think you'll fit in nicely with the culture here, but there's just one problem. You're a little too attractive and there are men here that I have the potential to mate with, and you're taking the attention away from me, so this just isn't going to work out." But that is the unspoken bias backed by findings.

How can we, as leaders, ensure that we are building the best teams we possibly can, independent of gender? In addition to building awareness of your gendered norms, it can also be helpful to rely on professional tools. Several companies provide services that remove biasing information from job descriptions and résumés to ensure potential candidates are getting a fair first look independent of their gender and the position for which you're hiring.

One such company, GapJumpers, recently found that only 20 percent of candidates who were anything other than white, able-bodied males made it to a first-round interview. But when potentially biasing elements in a résumé were hidden from a recruiter, the number jumped to 60 percent. So often, it's the little shortcuts our brains make that cause massive lost opportunities to hire the *right* person. For example, while a recruiter might be eager to hire a candidate who has identified himself as an Eagle Scout, is the recruiter excited because of the skill set that "Eagle Scout" confers, or is there a bias for a male leader? It's likely that the recruiter is truly trying to do the right thing, but if we don't replace the title of "Eagle Scout" with the related skill set that being a Scout entails, our brains are apt to take a shortcut and hire with a favorable male bias. Research consistently finds that, in comparable résumés, female names rather than male names are 40 percent less likely to get an interview.

In a study that's achieved some level of academic fame, U.S. orchestras in the 1970s and 1980s began using "blind audition" methods, whereby the candidates would perform behind a screen for the panelists. Researchers determined that this simple solution made it 50 percent more likely for a woman to advance to final rounds. While such elegant and simple solutions aren't always possible in our modern offices, the use of voice-changing software has become increasingly popular in interview rounds to guard against subtle or subconscious gender bias.

That may seem a little silly or extreme, but studies have found that low voices are judged to be more competent and trustworthy, creating yet another hurdle for females who tend to have higher-pitched voices.

What might be a better solution to traditional interviews? How about actually letting the candidates do the job they are applying for! GapJumpers finds that when candidates are offered an opportunity to compete against one another by completing job-related tasks *prior* to the reveal of their gender, nearly 60 percent of the top performers are female.

Better Together

We are all bound to the sex instinct, but that doesn't mean we have to be victims of it. In fact, we have a great opportunity to help fight gender bias by forming alliances with one another to help intervene in our instincts. Right now, if you were to ask any woman to name three things about herself that are amazing, or three accomplishments she achieved at work this week that she's proud of, you might find it difficult to get a response. Ancestrally, women weren't rewarded for standing out (except for their beauty), and voicing accomplishments that denote status would certainly have been challenging to our ancestral males (since status is the currency with which they compete). Female modesty has been reinforced and coded as the norm. As a result, when women violate this gender norm by acting self-confident or bragging about their accomplishments, they face a well-documented backlash in the workplace. Corinne Moss-Racusin, a psychology professor who studies gender norms, finds that women who talk about their accomplishments are less liked by their colleagues, earn less money, and are more likely to be passed over for advancement opportunities.

On the opposite spectrum, men who break gender normative behaviors by being vulnerable, displaying empathy, and exhibiting modesty are *also* penalized by colleagues with ratings of lower competency and capability. Additional research has found that men who are more warm, supportive, and agreeable make significantly less income (18 percent less, on average) compared to their more stereotypically masculine male colleagues.

The ability to recognize high-performing males and females who demonstrate humility and empathy should be a cornerstone of any organization looking to build an atmosphere of cooperation and collaboration (a topic we'll explore more in Chapter 5).

Here's one solution I like to share with the leaders and organizations with which I work: Help champion the status of anyone's accomplishments, regardless of gender, by encouraging colleagues to pair up with *brag buddies*. In order for a female not to experience the backlash of bragging about her own accomplishments, she should be paired with another individual in the organization who can share on her behalf. In this way, her value will be recognized without the negative ramifications.

Similarly, a gender-bias-breaking male's brag buddy can share how his humility helped save the company money or outperform a competitor so as to prevent the otherwise negative-status devaluation that comes with his non-gender-normative behavior. Brag buddies provide key opportunities for an organizational culture shift. They also allow those in non-gender-conforming roles to gain respect and attention for their accomplishments— and not just in a work environment but in society at large. Whether at a networking event or a friends and family outing, leaning on a brag buddy can help us all override the instinctual assignment of gender norms and instead begin celebrating individuals.

When I think back to my great-grandmother, who broke all kinds of generational norms, there's no denying how far we have come in a short one-hundred-year span. But we must recognize the ways in which our biology still pits us against the best version of ourselves, and of others, independent of gender. Awareness is the first step toward taking responsibility to intervene in this instinct.

Chapter 2: Key Takeaways

- Recognize how your own "hot" or "cold" emotional states might be affecting your decisions, or the decisions of others.
- Ask people you trust to challenge you whenever they hear you use gendered language.
- Take an Implicit Association Test to become more consciously aware of the subconscious associations you might have around gender (or other biases!): www.implicit.harvard.edu/implicit/taketest.html.
- Intentionally read books and listen to podcasts by women to challenge your perception and definition of leadership.
- Actively seek out parenting and housekeeping books and podcasts authored by men.
- Identify ways you might be misinterpreting sexual cues.
- Use gender-masking tools to limit gender bias throughout the hiring process.
- Find and use brag buddies.
- Be willing to intervene if you see a situation that might be sexual harassment.
- Review your company's sexual harassment policies to ensure they contain language about the freeze response.
- When in pursuit of a sexual partner, recognize that a smile does not imply consent. Understand

the freeze response and give time and space for
the other person to come back to you.

- If you've experienced the freeze response, recognize that your biology was trying to protect you.
  Release yourself from any blame you may have
  carried for not doing more in that moment.

CHAPTER 3

Variety

The Surprising Satisfaction of Less

Lessons from Lego

TAKE A MOMENT AND THINK about the most powerful brands and companies that are massively profitable. A few standards likely leap to mind: Apple. Google. Amazon. Ferrari. Lego.Okay, maybe a toy company didn't make it on your list. But between the years 2008 and 2010 the Lego Group, producers of the plastic molded toy bricks, was surpassing Apple's profits and by 2015, they had overtaken Ferrari as the world's most powerful brand. Quite a comeback for Lego, whose story almost ended back in 2003 when it found itself $800 million in debt.

How could a company that had never posted a loss, from its founding in 1932 through the late 1990s, have fallen so rapidly? And perhaps more importantly, how did they make such a stunning recovery?

Consultants in the late '90s had advised Lego leadership that they needed to diversify, insisting that the standard brick set was outdated. In following this advice, Lego began expanding its variety of bricks, creating complex pieces that were unique to highly specialized sets. Colors expanded from the classic red, yellow, and blue to include a palette of fifty. The brand even began selling clothes, jewelry, and a line of video games. Additionally, Lego built and operated theme parks, costing the company millions. All of this was a significant departure from Lego's standard plastic-injection brick set. By trying to cater to every market, they nearly ran the business to the ground. In 2000, Lego posted a $36 million loss. The core business was now a multi-layered jumble of ill-fitting pieces.

In 2003, Lego's vice president, Jørgen Vig Knudstorp, knew they were in trouble and didn't try to hide it. "We are on a burning platform," he told his colleagues. "We're running out of cash . . . [and] likely won't survive." Not exactly the most inspiring news to deliver to the board. But he had a plan. As Simon Cotterrell, part of the team at Interbrand, the company that manages the Lego brand, told *The Guardian* in a 2017 interview, the plan was to remind the team of their roots and what had made them so great to begin with. The continual outsourcing and ever-expanding variety wasn't the key to Lego's success.

They needed to return to keeping it simple and focusing on product quality rather than variety. As Cotterrell put it, the thinking was, "We're engineers. We know what we're good at. Let's stick to our knitting. [Which is] a very brave thing to do and it's where a lot of companies go wrong. They don't understand that—sometimes it's better to let go than to hang on."

But letting go is exactly what Vig Knudstorp set about doing. He slashed divisions where Lego had no expertise, selling off theme parks and video games, and simplified variety by bringing the number of individual pieces that were being manufactured at Lego back down to 6,500 (from upward of 13,000!). Before long, Lego was back on track.

The moral of the story: Just because you *can* do something doesn't mean that you should. It may sound trite, but it served to benefit Vig Knudstorp and the rest of the Lego team and ultimately their customers.

Surprisingly, having too many choices can create massive anxiety, dissatisfaction, and decision paralysis for countless numbers of us, every day. In fact, your instinct for *variety* may very well be to blame for, say, a loss of productivity, a failed relationship, or an overall sense of discontent. Many of us get trapped in the same cycle as the Lego Group, forgetting just how creative and productive we can be when we focus on what is already in our possession. But there are simple strategies to intervene in this instinct and discover the truth in how our brains really do perceive less as more.

Immediate Return Environments: Moving Beyond the Marshmallow

Every morning, when our ancestors woke up, they faced fairly binary decisions: *Should I leave the safety of my cave or stay inside? Should I hunt today or go hungry?* They had time to process their choices in context with their environments and come to sound conclusions. Our ancestors lived in an *immediate-return environment*. The decisions they made moment to moment had immediate impact on their survival and stress in ways that were easily measurable.

I'm hungry → I'll eat this hunk of meat
I'm thirsty → I'll search for water
I'm cold → I'll seek shelter

In their highly unpredictable environment, with limited choices, immediate-return decisions made sense. Behaviors like seeking shelter or food were reinforced immediately with positive or negative feedback.

I'm hungry → I'll eat this hunk of meat →
I no longer feel hungry

or

I'm hungry → I'll eat this hunk of meat → I'm ill → I will no longer eat meat that I find laying around → I'll hunt for fresh food instead

In the immediate-return environments of our ancestors, we got just that: an immediate return. We got the
feedback that our decision in that very moment was good
or bad. We lived completely in the present, which was a
good instinct in an unpredictable environment. Why
look too far ahead when things will likely change or I'm
unlikely to be around for it?

Scientific evidence suggests that this same evolutionary
framework underlies the high rate of teenage pregnancies
in environments where teens experience higher uncertainty and risk of early mortality. Researchers Margo
Wilson and Martin Daly of McMaster University describe
how between 1988 and 1993, homicide rates in Chicago var-
ied from neighborhood to neighborhood, with some
communities having one hundred times more murders
than others. Wilson and Daly's study found that when the
homicide rate was higher, women were having children at
a younger age, perhaps discounting their futures and the
likelihood of having later opportunities for reproduction.

The "marshmallow tests," a series of now-famous experiments conducted at Stanford University in the 1970s,
examined children's ability to override the instinct for im-
pulsive, immediate-return decision-making. Subjects
three to five years of age were presented with a marshmallow and told that if they didn't eat it, their reward
would double in the form of two marshmallows or pret-
zel sticks (depending upon their preferences). The
experimenter left the room for varying amounts of time
(up to fifteen minutes), and then returned. Children who

were able to delay their gratification doubled their payouts. Only a small number of children ate the marshmallow right away. The primary difference between children who engaged in immediate gratification versus those who were able to delay lies in their *perception of environmental stability.*

Fascinatingly, among the children who discounted their futures, had low socioeconomic status, or had poor trust (all factors that would suggest a perception of *low* environmental stability), a significantly higher number ate the marshmallow soon after the experimenter left the room. It seems they couldn't look forward to see a future in which they would get a reward, so they ate the treat that was in front of them. Their immediate-return decision probably looked something like this:

> There is a marshmallow in the room now that I can eat → I may not have another opportunity to eat this marshmallow → I will eat it now

When life doesn't hold many guarantees, there is a risk associated with investing beyond the present moment. These children were operating from an immediate-return environment mindset. In other words, their survival instinct was in full control.

A 2011 follow-up of the original participants of the Marshmallow Test found that those children who had been able to delay gratification demonstrated a more active prefrontal cortex than those who'd opted for immediate gratification—even forty years later! This suggests children who could delay gratification were operating with cognitive power that overrode their survival instinct. Follow-up experiments found that the children who were able to defer rewards also had higher SAT scores, healthier body mass indexes, and longer life expectancy.

If we are capable of overriding survival responses in circumstances when we truly believe the reward is forthcoming (in a short time frame), then why does our brain continually undermine our attempts at longer term success? For one, immediate gratification just feels good. It's a shot of dopamine to the brain. And the more time between a decision and its reward, the more difficulty your brain has in making the "right" choice now, for a better payoff later.

Think about the last diet you tried. You were probably all-in the first few days, but then your enthusiasm wavered. By day three, when you didn't get that immediate reward of stepping on the scale to see the numbers drop, or your waistband still felt snug, the time frame simply became too long for a delayed gratification response. From there we start justifying: *Why not eat that bagel? It doesn't seem to make a difference if I do or don't.* And what about that investment? *I've been putting it away to go to college, get a better job, buy a house, but the money is sitting there NOW! Maybe I should just buy that car? Or take that trip?*

Your choices and the predictability of your environment are intimately linked. If we have trustworthy information that delaying *now* will lead to higher payoff *later*, most of us can override our survival brain–immediate gratification mindset pretty well. But there's another factor that can derail delayed gratification: We have a more difficult time overriding our survival-obsessed, immediate gratification brain when our options *expand*.

Imagine I offer you a brownie for dessert. You politely decline. But then I show you the buffet. There are brownies, of course, but also pies, cookies, cakes, candies, and ice cream. Now, you're far more likely to indulge in dessert. You may even justify that the cookie you chose was at least healthier than the brownie I'd offered you. Your inability to resist dessert isn't a personal failure; it's because our brains aren't built for juggling delayed-return decisions in which there's an abundance of variety. Saying "no" or "yes" to any one thing is difficult enough, but with the expansion in variety, now you're not just saying no to a dessert (or a partner, or a job, or any other singular offer category), but to each and every option nested within that category. Let's return to the example I gave above for our ancestors in a highly unpredictable world with limited choices:

> I'm hungry → I'll eat this hunk of meat →
> I no longer feel hungry

or

> I'm hungry → I'll eat this hunk of meat →
> I'm ill → I will no longer eat meat that I find lying
> around → I'll hunt fresh food instead

Part of the reason that our decisions were so easy in the ancestral environment is that they were *limited*. Imagine the scenario above with a buffet of meats to choose from. What if you fell ill? Would you risk the meat the next time or go hunting? Or try a different type of meat? What if all meat makes you sick? Or berries? What if when you hunted you had the choice to use arrows, guns, traps, poison, or crossbows and you'd had some success with large prey with firepower, but also some misses. When you add variety, decisions quickly get complicated for the simple reason that variety itself is an immediately rewarded pleasurable experience. In other words, our brains crave it!

Contemporary Choice

Our variety instinct was a good thing for our ancestors. They needed this instinct to ensure all their eggs weren't in one basket (quite literally when it came to reproduction), and to eat an optimal diet ensuring that all of their nutritional needs were met. An insignificant amount of choice combined with an immediate-return environment allowed our ancestors to enjoy and quickly learn how variety often yielded positive outcomes.

But the sparse environment of our ancestors looked nothing like the bustling metropolises of today, where you can't spin in a circle without landing in a fast food joint with hundreds of options, or where a potential new mate is as near as a swipe on an app on your mobile device, or where your decisions at work all begin with determining which projects require your immediate attention and which can be de-prioritized. In a world of nearly unlimited choices—many with returns that are significantly delayed—we are suddenly facing real challenges.

In fact, the average human makes about thirty-five thousand decisions per day. Think about when you first woke up: *Should I hit the snooze button? Work out? Eat oatmeal or Cheerios? Eggs. How many? With cheese? What kind? Olive oil or avocado? Maybe butter. Should I put skim or almond milk in my coffee?*

A study from Cornell University found that we make 227 decisions every day on food alone and our instincts are doing us no favors here. Remember a time when you were really craving ice cream. Once you got over the dilemma of having to choose which flavor you wanted, relive that first, enchanting taste of cold, creamy sweetness. That hit is incredible! But by the time you finish the cone, you likely aren't enjoying that flavor nearly as much. That's because we are naturally primed to have "sensory-specific satiety," a mechanism that triggers us to "move on from that nutrient." It's when you say: I've had enough—what's next on the menu?

This was useful to our ancestors because it ensured they were eating a variety of foods and not just trying to subsist on blueberries. But what happens today, when, after that vanilla cone, we can just move on to the chocolate? Or the caramel flavor. Oh, and how about French fries!

Our instinct for variety is so strong, researchers find that humans tend to eat *four times* as much food when there are multiple options to choose from. The flavors don't even have to be distinct. Differently shaped pasta is all it takes to spark the drive to consume more, as our palate enjoys the variety of textures!

But our instinct for variety isn't restricted to food. The choices, options, and seemingly endless variety of tasks we have on our plates at work can ultimately prevent us from making good choices—or any choice at all!

How often have you sat at your desk for an hour or more with a list of twenty things you needed to do that day only to spend the first hour of your morning procrastinating or stuck in decision paralysis? You didn't know which task to choose to start with and so you just never started.

Equally disastrous is when we attempt several tasks at once. We try to tackle every item on our to-do list, while attending to each request that pops up in our emails. We bounce from one task to the next, trying to get everything done. But multitasking is a myth. MIT neuroscientist Earl K. Miller states it bluntly: "Multitasking is not humanly possible." When we attempt to multitask we make more errors, we are less creative, and our productivity plummets. Humans don't operate like machines; we have a limited amount of cognitive bandwidth. And while we want to believe that we can take it all on, sometimes it's best to establish restrictions.

In fact, leading research supports that establishing constraints, such as budget and time deadlines, can actually increase our creativity and the number of solutions that we develop for solving problems and designing or building products. Limiting possibilities helps our brains to focus and provides a creativity boost. Instead of allowing your bandwidth to be drained in every direction with a seemingly endless variety of daily tasks, establish constraints in your work by setting timers for particular activities, internet research, or brainstorming.

Choice, in the ancestral environment, was always a positive option. Choice meant some level of abundance and predictability. Perhaps this is why so many of us allowed panic to sink in when we saw grocery shelves bare of essentials like toilet paper and flour at the start of the COVID-19 pandemic. It signaled some upheaval in the environment that we had come to recognize as stable and certain. But counterintuitively, under non-pandemic shortage conditions, more choice in the context of our modern environment can sometimes create an anxious frame of mind rather than a blissful one. The very word "decide" shares an etymological root with the word "homicide." Caedere, killing or cutting down choices, can be excruciating for humans. We hate narrowing our opportunities, even when our own fear of not making the "right" decision prevents us from making one at all. Opportunities become trade-offs in this mindset. The positive potential of one decision translates into the costs of not choosing another. While our instinct for variety is infinite, our ability to *manage* the variety we crave is limited. When we are presented with too many choices, we often avoid making decisions altogether.

Worse yet, when we do make decisions, they aren't as satisfying if we have numerous choices. In one study from Columbia and Stanford Universities, researchers found that when subjects were confronted with twenty-four to thirty options, they were significantly less satisfied with their final choice than those participants who had just six options to choose from.

Our *fear* of making the wrong choice boils down to simple math. When given just two possibilities, we have a fifty-fifty chance of making the "right" choice. Or perhaps even slightly higher than 50 percent if we consider that both options probably have some positive outcomes or might be equal in the opportunities they present. But when the choice field broadens to include twenty choices, suddenly our chance of making the "right" choice drops to a mere 5 percent! While this math obviously isn't a perfect equation, our brains treat it as such. We focus on the opportunities *lost* rather than enjoying the present choice we've made, leaving us in a state of perpetual dissatisfaction, which compounds our constant primal urge to chase the *next* shiny object.

When you're trapped in a hedonistic cycle of looking for ever-greener pastures, you're in a no-win situation known as the *abundance paradox*. In the modern world, where the possibility of a new or better job, home, or mate is just one click away, we are swiping ourselves right into unhappiness.

I Can't Get No Satisfaction:
The Abundance Paradox

According to a Gallup report, a majority of Americans (52.3 percent) are unhappy at work. A number of surveys has been conducted on happiness at work, but sadly it doesn't appear that any has a less grim outlook. Our slide into dissatisfaction has been relatively steady since the Conference Board conducted their initial survey on job satisfaction and found a peak (61.1 percent satisfied) back in 1987. But would changing jobs actually lead to more satisfaction? Not until we can convince our variety-lusting brains that more choice doesn't mean *better* choice. In fact, many of us find ourselves continually chasing a different job, a nicer car, a more attractive mate—all in search of more and "better" variety.

Consider our nation's obsessive collecting of things. While science has repeatedly shown that people often feel overwhelmed or depressed by having too many possessions to maintain, we still buy and consume at unprecedented rates. For our ancestors, owning a variety of objects denoted status and power, and conveyed a level of safety and stability. Just like the children who were able to resist the temptation to eat the marshmallow right away showed a healthy abundance mindset, those ancestors who could maintain a collection of things demonstrated their ability to live beyond an immediate-return environment. But once again, our ancestral environment was substantially more sparse than the consumer world in which we currently reside. Ancestrally, the instinct to collect and show off such wealth could have been to the great benefit of those with the most stuff.

In a great ironic twist of this instinct today, we find our bookshelves stuffed to the brim with the latest Marie Kondo titles on how to tidy up, with few of us actually reaping the beneficial advice inside. We like the idea of simplifying, but our instinct for variety fights the urge to let go.

Another example of the variety instinct gone awry: The fact that 50 percent of marriages end in divorce is not a statistic that should be surprising to anyone who understands mating systems in the context of the abundance paradox. The shocking fact is that 50 percent of marriages actually last! While the institution of marriage came into popularity in the 1300s, it is still a relatively modern concept to our Stone Age brains, which operate as if mating opportunities were severely limited.

The Coolidge Effect owes its name to an illustrious incident, when President Coolidge and Mrs. Coolidge were separately visiting a chicken farm on the same day. Mrs. Coolidge noted the vigor and excitement that a rooster exhibited when pursuing hens, and she reportedly asked the tour guide to be sure to point this out to Mr. Coolidge. When the guide relayed this exchange to the president later that afternoon, he replied, "Tell Mrs. Coolidge that there is more than one hen." Point being: The variety instinct drives males in particular (but females as well) to often seek opportunities to mate outside of their primary partner. While a woman could mate with 100 men and produce only one offspring, a man could mate with 100 women and have the potential for 100 offspring. Our biology confirms the rewards: a plethora of studies demonstrate increased ejaculate volume, sperm motility, and likelihood of conception when men have extra-pair copulations.

The male propensity to seek variety in mates is commonly known, but what's the ancestral advantage for a female to do the same? Paternal confusion was a strategy that women used to great advantage to obtain resources and cooperation from multiple males. Without the modern tools of paternity tests, the only way a man could be certain that a child was not his was if he hadn't mated with its mother. Paternity confusion was a strategy that allowed a woman to convince multiple men to invest in her offspring. If a man couldn't be sure whether or not a child was his, he would be more likely to offer protection and other resources on the chance he was helping out his genetic progeny.

So, in the ancestral environment, appetite for sexual variety was advantageous to both sexes. But now, we live in a world of 8 billion people and near-limitless choice and accessibility to potential mates. Some dating apps boast that their members make over sixteen thousand swipes per second! Our brains are overstimulated by such staggering choices. If we are eventually capable of making a decision to "match" with a mate on one of these sites, it's typically not to the preclusion of others. This level of choice eases the pain of loss aversion that we might otherwise face. But by "leaving the door open" (for many others to walk in), we never fully invest in the partner we've selected.

More matches, more right swipes, are never far and the pool of potential mates is practically bottomless. Abundance makes it far too easy to fall into hedonistic tendencies to chase something better—or at least different. We mistakenly believe that the *next* thing will save us, the next thing will be better, the next partner, project, job will bring true happiness. But that's just your Stone Age brain guiding you to act on outdated instincts.

How Maximizing May Be Minimalizing Our Chances of Real Success

The late behavioral economist Herbert Simon describes our tendency to look to the next thing as potentially better as *maximizing*. People who maximize are always wondering what other choice might have been better or might have made them happier.

For maximizers, the "good enough" point of reference is always shifting. In the context of a seemingly endless array of "swipes" available, that great first date can suddenly seem, well, not nearly as satisfying as it might be with the *next* match. The job that was so great the first two weeks is now just okay, and soon we're scrolling through job-hunting sites on a quest to find the one that will *really* be satisfying. Every alternative we encounter changes our reference point of what *could* be. The more choices we make, the more that reference point shifts, and we find ourselves literally swiping our productivity and health right into the garbage.

As a teenager, I struggled to choose the colleges to which I wanted to apply. I spent hours looking through literature on colleges and universities of all sizes, in all areas of the world, with all different opportunities and aspects that made each uniquely enticing. It seemed that I had more choices of where to apply than I had time to explore, and next to zero information or understanding of how any one option would be better than another. But then my grandmother, quite wisely, told me: "Don't let your options be your burdens."

Her simple outlook on the situation was more powerful than I think she ever realized. My reference point had been shifting with every potential opportunity. Once I'd accepted the idea of one college, I was looking out from that choice and thinking about all the others and how I might have chosen better, rather than looking inward at all the positive things about the choice I had made. I was engaging in maximizing behaviors and it was getting me nowhere.

What my grandmother was suggesting, and what Herbert Simon and modern behavioral economists like Barry Schwartz would support, is that people are happier when they become *satisficers* instead of maximizers. Satisficers spend less time worrying about all the choices they might make and alternatives they might have and instead adopt a standard set of "good enough." When faced with a decision, they accept a choice that meets the criteria—without agonizing over finding an absolute, ultimate "perfect" fit.

Satisficers' decisions are based in the knowledge that they have about acceptable outcomes, and then their point of reference doesn't shift with every new option. Either the option meets the threshold criteria and it's selected, or it doesn't and that option is discarded. What knowledge did I have about colleges? Plenty! I just wasn't referencing the right sources. I was trying to evaluate the best option based on external factors (a college's reputation, where my friends were going, what would be acceptable to my parents) rather than asking myself if *I'd* enjoy my choice. What factors were important to me? Did it meet *my* needs? What were those needs? I needed to list them out explicitly. Then, if a college checked the boxes, it was an *excellent* choice, independent of any other potentially excellent choices. I wasn't going to get anywhere further by stewing on the myriad of "what if" situations. My trying to maximize the decision meant I would inevitably look back on it with regret or disappointment, no matter which college I chose.

Know When You've Kissed Enough Frogs

Dr. Dermot Jevens, a veterinary surgical specialist in South Carolina and co-founder of the national award-winning Upstate Veterinary Specialists practice, describes his satisficing philosophy on hiring: "I lay out a clear definition of what qualifications I am looking for ahead of time. As soon as those assets clearly match a candidate, I hire them. It doesn't matter if it is the first day of the candidate review process. I don't need or want to interview three other candidates 'just in case.' You have to kiss a few frogs, but sometimes the first frog you kiss turns into a prince or princess. No reason to keep looking past that." (Full disclosure, I'm a huge fan of this philosophy for reasons beyond business. After first meeting Dr. Jevens on an airplane, he and I quickly assessed there was no need to look further. We have been happily together ever since.)

Think about the last time you went to a fancy restaurant for dinner. Did you agonize over the menu? After all, you wanted to make sure you had a great meal—that you maximized this opportunity. And did you fully enjoy your choice, or were you distracted by comparing and wondering if your dinner partner's dish might have been better? Maximizers use their relative positioning as an assessment of their own decision's value and worth, which often lands them into a continuous, unsatisfactory chase. And there are plenty of variations on the theme:

"Wonder what else is on right now."
"Sure, this product has a 91 percent approval rating
     on Amazon, but what does *Consumer Reports*
     have to say?"

> "Are you certain you want to go to *this* Chinese res-
> taurant? Yelp says the one across town has
> better wontons."

If this sounds like you, you might have maximizing tendencies. Don't worry, nothing wrong with that. But in a world in which variety is ever expanding, researching every option in order to select the *ultimate* best one simply isn't realistic. When alternatives are burgeoning, it *feels* as if there must be a perfect option. This feeling causes an increase in your expectations, ultimately leading to a higher probability of disappointment with whatever decision you make.

One might assume that acting as a satisficer leads to a compromised or average life. The reality is quite the opposite. Researchers from Swarthmore and the University of Pennsylvania established a scale to assess how well-being correlated to one's tendencies to maximize versus satisfice. Their results demonstrated that subjects who behaved with satisficing tendencies had significantly more life satisfaction, happiness, optimism and self-esteem, and significantly less regret and depression, than those with maximizing tendencies.

Another study published in *Psychological Science* found that recent college graduates who ranked higher on the maximizing scale selected and accepted jobs that paid an average of 20 percent higher salaries than their peers who had scored higher on the satisficing scale. And yet, these same maximizers felt *less satisfied* in their new roles, despite the higher pay. Why? Maximizers rely more heavily on external criterion to determine the "optimal" choice.

But what does optimal *mean*? And who decides? "Best" and "optimal" are imprecise measures that can shift with any new perspective. How do you know you have the *best* without comparing every alternative? You don't. And frankly you can't.

Our variety instinct unconsciously leads us to believe that there is always something better, always a greener pasture to chase after. I'm not endorsing the idea that a long-term commitment to a single restaurant, career, or life partner is the only or best option for everyone. But what is clear is that we need to be aware of the influence the variety instinct holds over us so we can ensure that this powerful imperative doesn't lead us toward professional and personal dissatisfaction.

FOMO No MO(re)

The antidote to the abundance paradox, is surprisingly simple: *Lust after what you already have.*

We have to start recognizing that good enough really is *great*! Apply this motto generously in your life, whether it's the mundane choices you make daily about what you're going to have for dinner or the bigger decisions about your job or your marriage. Here are three steps you can follow any time you're facing a decision with a multitude of choices in order to ensure you're acting like a satisficer:

1. **CREATE A DETAILED LIST OF CRITERIA THAT
   MEET YOUR ACCEPTABILITY THRESHOLD.** Not
   an extrinsic measure of what will bring
   you the most money or the most status or
   what others say is the best choice for you.
   Rather, explicitly list the standards that the
   "right" decision needs to meet in order for
   you to feel good about it.

For example, when Dr. Jevens sits down to interview
a candidate for an opening in his practice, he has a check-
list of all the qualifications he's looking for: (1) Do they
have the correct, up-to-date licensing and qualifications
for the role? (2) Do they understand and demonstrate the
mission and core values of the hospital? (3) Can they give
examples of how they worked through a difficult situation with a client? (4) Do they value honesty and
integrity?

Whatever the qualifications for your decision, write
them down. Spend enough time to ensure that you've
listed everything you know you'll need in order to feel
good about making this choice. Ask yourself: "Will
meeting these standards make me happy?" rather than,
"Is this the *best* I can do?"

2. **MAKE YOUR DECISION NONREVERSIBLE.**
   Studies have found that when we buy
   something with a no-refund policy, we are
   less likely to regret our purchase.

In fact, we begin to exhibit something known as *choice-supportive bias* (also called "post-purchase rationalization"). In choice-supportive bias we exaggerate the positive features of the item we selected and exacerbate the flaws in the option we didn't choose. Here, I want you to go *all-in* with your decision—and set a time frame. For example, before you convince yourself that you need a new job, a new spouse, or a new home, try being all-in for thirty days exactly where you already are. Imagine how good you'll feel when you lust after what's already yours. When you establish a thirty-day practice, you give your brain the opportunity to realize that, realistically, you aren't going to mate with *every* potential person out there, or find a better job every other month.

Imagine what you'd do if you were already happy in your job, relationship, or home? Maybe you would show up early to work. Or you'd bring your beloved flowers. Perhaps if you were already happy in your home, you'd enjoy the rooms you have and work to make them even more special? Commit to doing those actions. Schedule them into your day: *Day one: I'm taking my wife to dinner. Day two: I'm texting her a random compliment at 12 p.m. Day three: I'll fix that door hinge that she always complains is squeaky.*

Rabbi Hyman Schachtel declared in 1954 that "happiness is not having what you want, but wanting what you have"—a sentiment that has since been echoed widely, from philosophers to country music legend Garth Brooks.

Go all-in with your full focus on whatever it is you want, *as if* it was your only option, and soon, the alternative grass you thought was looking so green will likely start to show its spots.

3. **REPEAT.** Variety may be the spice of life, but it's an instinct that would have us so drowned in the spices that we wouldn't recognize the natural flavor of our original choice. We must continually reframe our lust for the things we *already* have as if they were our only option. This will help us rein in our runaway instinct.

Going All-in with Five Guys

A great case study of these methods comes from the massively successful Five Guys burger franchise. Founded in 1986 by husband and wife Jerry and Janie Murrell, Five Guys was ahead of the curve. In an age of expanding menus catering to our instinctive drive for variety, Five Guys held firm to a minimalistic style. The Murrells founded the company with a few basic principles and they were clear about measures of success. In a recent *Forbes* interview, Jerry, the patriarch of five sons (the "Five Guys") who all help run the company, said, "The only thing we did right was stick to our guns." Their principles included: no delivery, no advertisements, no complicated menus, and nothing frozen. These were nonnegotiable business decisions. And the Murrells went *all-in*.

Even as demand for milkshakes from customers remained steady, the Murrells resisted because: *nothing frozen*. In spite of the demands coming from the Pentagon to deliver a few burgers to keep the country's best and brightest defense workers satiated, they stuck to their policy: no delivery. When staffers came up with a campaign to send newly elected President Obama a Five Guys' T-shirt, it was an immediate-return decision that would have provided tons of free press. But Murrell fell back to his decision criteria: no advertising. Five Guys would stick to their guns and rely only on word of mouth. (As a side note, Obama visited a Five Guys soon after and ate a classic burger in front of a cadre of video cameras and press.)

The Murrells' efforts to fight the abundance paradox speaks to the company's success. Five Guys ranked first in "Fast Food: Large Chains" and "Best Burger" in Zagat's 2011 annual Fast Food Survey, first in "burger, steak, chicken and grill" category in a 2016 Market Force UK survey, and has enjoyed a growth upward of 32.8 percent.

Less truly might be more.

The next time you feel your variety instinct tugging your sleeve toward greener, better, more, more, more— remember how much you can build with a simple beef patty, or four colored Lego bricks. Stop kissing every frog. You might already have your prince of a partner, idea, job, life—or even just a burger—right in front of you.

Chapter 3: Key Takeaways

- Check your assumption that more is always better.
- Cut or limit your choices by establishing constraints and enacting deadlines.
- Recognize that we don't always live in an immediate return environment. Be willing to delay gratification for a better return at a slightly later time.
- Make the "right" choice *now*, for a better payoff later.
- Lust after what you already have.
- Define your acceptability threshold and don't kiss any more frogs than you need to!
- Go all-in; make decisions irreversible.

Self-Deception

I Know You Are But What Am I?

Of Two Minds

Starting in the 1940s up until the early '70s, doctors experimented with a complex, last-ditch medical procedure called a corpus callostomy on a small handful of patients who suffered from severe epileptic seizures. During the roughly ten-hour surgery, surgeons would carefully slice through a patient's corpus callosum, the structure that connects the left and right hemispheres of the brain, thereby disconnecting the two sides of their neocortex, the region that governs language, motor control, and conscious thought. This risky surgery stopped the seizures and gave patients their lives back. But there was a serious side effect: They were now literally of two minds, with each brain hemisphere operating completely independent of the other.

Words, objects, or pictures presented to one side of a patient's brain went unnoticed by the other side, as neuroscience researchers Michael Gazzaniga and Roger Sperry discovered. We know that the left hemisphere of the brain largely controls the right side of the body, and that the left side of the body is largely controlled by the right hemisphere. But in their now famous "Split-Brain Experiments," Gazzaniga and Sperry ascertained that the left and right hemispheres had specialized functions. For example, the left hemisphere is responsible for verbal ability; and while the right hemisphere could understand input, split-brain patients were unable to verbalize what they'd seen or been told if it had been given *only* to the right hemisphere.

Here's the fascinating part: When Gazzaniga and Sperry told a subject's right brain, for instance, to go for a walk (in this case, by showing their left eye a flash card that commanded them to "get up and walk"), the left brain would construct a justification for why they were suddenly walking. Remember, the left side of the brain had never actually *seen* the card commanding them to walk, so the logical response when the experimenter asked, "Why are you walking?" might have been "I don't know." But instead, the test subjects provided justifications for the behaviors they were engaged in, such as:

"I'm stretching my legs," or "I'm thirsty, so I'm going to walk over there to get a Coke."

Is the subject telling the truth? Is he really thirsty? Or was this just a lie to justify an action the left brain couldn't explain? If the left hemisphere had seen the command to walk, and it fabricated the lie that the subject was thirsty, then it would be an intentional lie. But the left hemisphere never had access to the command to walk. So is his answer that he's thirsty *still* a lie? The split-brained patients continually gave confident false answers to the experimenter's question, rather than saying "I don't know." They didn't realize they were lying, they were simply constructing stories that justified their actions.

While this might sound bizarre and straight out of the pages of a science fiction novel, the reality is we are all continuously doing the exact same thing. We often take actions based on motives directed by our subconscious minds, and then we consciously justify our behaviors.

Neuroscientist Benjamin Libet first demonstrated this powerful subconscious "choice" in the early 1980s, and his work has been repeated by dozens of other researchers. Libet wired participants to an EEG machine, which measures electromagnetic activity in the brain. Subjects were then asked to make a simple hand gesture at their own volition. Libet observed that while the conscious awareness of the decision to move the hand preceded the actual motion of the hand by about 200 milliseconds, there was measurable electrical activity in the brain, demonstrating an unconscious decision to move the hand, a full 350 milliseconds before the conscious awareness was indicated. In other words, the subconscious mind had made the decision, informed the conscious mind of its intent, and the motions were then completed 550 milliseconds after the initial intention as indicated by electrical actions of the subconscious brain. Your subconscious is making almost all of your choices for you, before you even are aware of it.

Twenty years later, using fMRI (functional magnetic resonance imaging) to more accurately monitor brain activity, a similar experiment was conducted by scientists at the Max Planck Institute for Human Cognitive and Brain Sciences. Participants were asked to push a button at their own pace using either their right or left hand, to be decided by the participant. They were also instructed to mark the time at which they had made the decision to push the button. The eerie finding was that the researchers could study a subject's brain activity and accurately predict which hand she would use, a full seven seconds prior to the participant herself being aware of the decision!

The conscious brain "decided" to push the button only after the subconscious decided to do so. Just like the split-brained patients, we construct stories to justify our actions without ever being aware of an underlying motive—in our case, the suggestions made by our subconscious minds.

Intent to Deceive

It's a universal human instinct—whether your brain hemi-spheres are intact or not—to engage in self-justification of behaviors without a deep, more fully aware under-standing of why we are enacting them. In other words, as humans we are hardwired to lie and self-deceive, to others and to ourselves.

This might seem antithetical to our primary goal of survival. After all, isn't knowing exactly where you stand of the utmost importance?

Then again, imagine if your ancestors were armed with complete and full self-knowledge of their relatively limited abilities (*I can make fire and procreate, but I'm a lousy hunter and protector of my family*). Then consider their chances in the heavily loaded odds (*tigers, snakes, harsh winters, that shifty neighbor*) against their daily sur-vival. Not the most motivating imagery to get anyone leaping from their caves with glee to greet the day and all the challenges it brings.

Nature is a beast, unrelenting in her abuse. When you think about it, you are a miracle. An absurdly, statistically improbable miracle that only exists because of hundreds of thousands of years during which your ancestors overes-timated their skills, competencies, intelligence, and beauty, allowing them to forge ahead and overcome challenges.

You may think you are a pretty accurate judge of your own behaviors and abilities, but it's also likely that you are just a good liar (even if it's unintentional). *Believing* you're better than you are gives you the edge you need to actually be a bit better—just as it gave our ancestors an edge at overcoming terrible odds of survival.

As economist Robin Hanson explains it, the conscious mind is not a CEO, but rather, a press secretary that's better off not fully knowing the deeper reasons behind our actions. After all, such information might make it more difficult to convincingly justify our behaviors and achieve that consonance our brain so dearly craves. Our conscious mind adopts an active avoidance of evidence that might prevent it from telling the story it has crafted. Consider the following series of questions:

> Would you voluntarily make an unethical choice?
> Would you agree that voluntarily breaking the law
>   is unethical?
> Do you think you are an unethical person?
> Have you driven on the highway in the past few
>   weeks?
> Did you exceed the speed limit?

If you're like most people, you answered that of course voluntarily breaking the law is unethical and, as an ethical person, something you wouldn't do! Then when you realized that you might have been doing a few (or more than a few) miles per hour over the posted speed limit on the highway you likely dismissed the un-ethical behavior by justifying it: "*Everyone* goes a little over the limit." (*Insert parental voice here making the state-*

*ment that just because everyone jumps off a bridge, doesn't
mean you should too.)*

Our penchant for fables and their justification was a
beneficial tool for our ancestors, in many ways. In the extremely social context in which they lived, lying allowed
them the ability to exploit others whose goals conflicted
with their own. For example, if I could convince you that
I was indeed the best hunter in the tribe, I might be able
to elicit a better return on a trade. You might believe that
I'd make a better mate than another whose hunting skills
aren't as good as mine. And I might be able to justify the
lie to myself by thinking: *Well, technically, I am a better
provider. Sure, that was in fact Joseph's meat that I stole, but
since he didn't notice, I'm clearly better suited to provide.*

There is little doubt that deception was a powerful
shaping force on our behaviors. If we got away with it, deception could convey huge benefits to our survival and
potentially even increase our mating opportunities. But
if we got caught and lost the trust of the tribe or were
ousted—that would prove devastating, if not deadly.

Unfortunately, in a modern world, our subconscious
minds don't always make the best choices for us. Our instinct for self-deceit has the power to wreck our
relationships and professional lives. For example, we
build self-deceptive stories and justifications largely as a
result of a concept known as *cognitive dissonance,* a tension that is caused by two incongruent truths being held
at the same time. Cognitive dissonance can cause significant mental turmoil. For example, you might know that:

- Smoking is terribly dangerous and causes lung cancer.
- You still smoke a pack a day.

Neuroscientists have found that in this state of dissonance, the reasoning areas of the brain shut down, only to be restored with the emotional happiness we feel as we resolve and restore harmony through conscious justification. For example, in the above scenario, you might self-delude by thinking to yourself, "Smoking is terribly dangerous and causes lung cancer and I smoke a pack a day, *but* I'm healthy and exercise a lot so I'm not at risk."

Studies consistently show that we overrate ourselves on measures of physical attractiveness, generosity, IQ, leadership, and even driving ability. Our self-deception can even have health consequences. Lying is known to make us physically sick! "Research has linked telling lies to an increased risk of cancer, increased risk of obesity, anxiety, depression, addiction, gambling, poor work satisfaction, and poor relationships," says Dr. Deirdre Lee Fitzgerald, professor of psychology at Eastern Connecticut State University. We suffer mentally and physically when we consciously lie. But evolution created a workaround: Deceive ourselves *first*.

Self-deception not only dodges some of the personal costs of suppressing truths, but if we truly believe we are being honest, we are far better at convincing others. As science historian Oren Harman so eloquently explains, "We have evolved a brain architecture that allows self-deception to do whatever is right by us. Sometimes the truth is worth concealing, especially from ourselves."

Rendering lies unconscious removes cues that others might pick up on, alerting them to our deceit. The forces that keep us from recognizing some dangerous truth about ourselves are so powerful, they have often become fodder for parody. For instance, the homophobic male who drives a big truck, cusses, and is a proverbial "man's man"? Turns out there is scientific evidence demonstrating that this exact archetype is more likely to be aroused by homosexual porn.

Sometimes deception is so deep that others buy into it at a significant cost to themselves. Elizabeth Holmes was a Silicon Valley darling. As a nineteen-year-old Stanford dropout she quickly earned the trust of major corporations, world leaders, and the media alike, while gracing the covers of *Forbes*, *Fortune*, and *Inc*. Holmes was poised to take on the health care industry with her disruptive start-up company, Theranos. Her claim that she possessed the technology to run hundreds of common health tests on a few drops of blood had won her company a $9 billion valuation. The only problem was that the technology only existed in the mind of Elizabeth Holmes. Her $9 billion company was smoke and mirrors—based on nothing but deception. Even as the façade of Theranos began to crumble around her and charges of fraud from the Securities and Exchange Commission landed her a $500,000 fine, Holmes still held on to her truth that, despite all evidence to the contrary, her technology was valid.

Dr. Dan Ariely, a professor of psychology and behavioral economics at Duke, suggests that, in part, this is likely what made Holmes so successful to begin with. Ariely's work reveals that when people tell lies repeatedly, their brains become less reactive to that lie. In short, he says, "We start believing our own lies."

To be clear, self-deception isn't just a defensive tool. In ancestral times, undue confidence paid dividends in attracting allies, mates, and resources. Radiating confidence (rather than painting a more accurate picture) still builds genuine confidence. Those who appear strong in difficult times are highly desired as mates and, therefore, the genes for self-deception continue to be selected. Forget realism: The better our ancestors were at shielding themselves from the woes that actually defined their reality, the more their self-created placebo took the shape of reality.

Power of Placebo—Helpful Deception

The placebo effect is perhaps the most famous example of self-deception, and its effects have engrossed scientists for decades. Typically, the placebo effect is studied by having participants consume a pill with zero biologically relevant effects (often dubbed a "sugar pill"), and testing the results of this pill against both control and experimental groups. Biologically ineffective placebos often turn out to be as effective, if not *more* effective, than pills with active biological relevancy. Research shows that the placebo effect can help people to lose weight, reduce blood pressure, lower pain, mediate nausea, and even regrow hair. The placebo effect is so powerful that a 2008 study published by the *British Medical Journal* found that nearly half of American doctors regularly prescribe placebos to their patients. A 2013 follow-up study in *PLOS One* found even higher usage of placebos among general practitioners (97 percent), with the majority of these doctors (77 percent) prescribing placebos at least once a week. If you've ever been prescribed antibiotics for a virus, a treatment that provides no scientifically valid relief for viral conditions, then you have been given a placebo. While it may make us question the ethics of doctors, it's hard to complain when the outcomes are typically positive. Our brains believe the stories we tell—even the stories about our medications.

Thankfully, the placebo effect can also provide us with a counterintuitive way to hack our self-deception instinct for better results. Think of what happens to people who consistently tell themselves that they are tired, unmotivated, a failure. They're effectively taking a placebo pill that ensures those results. More often than not, they prove themselves right because they've set the trap of either having to (1) consciously recognize that they're lying to themselves (which is incredibly difficult to do given how much our biology fights to keep our lies hidden), or (2) fulfill the behaviors that reinforce their statements.

Instead of falling into this trap, we can all try to put a positive spin on our lies. Tell yourself, for example, "I'm an excellent public speaker." You might not be, but when you've consciously voiced it, even if only in your own private thoughts, you've taken the sugar pill that promises better public speaking skills. The more you convince yourself, the more comfortable you'll be with the lie, and the more you'll be able to convince others of it. In other words, your confidence will win the day and reinforce your original lie. It *becomes* the truth.

Harvard philosopher William James called this belief in self, "precursive faith." I call it *action to drive belief*. Instead of relying on the evidence that our conscious brain relays *from* our subconscious beliefs, we must drive the evidence consciously by taking action first and nudging our subconscious belief toward change. When we consciously adopt the behavior and actions of the person we want to believe we are, we consciously control our press secretary. Our conscious mind drives the report back to our subconscious: This *is* who we are.

Dr. Nick Morgan, a top communication theorist and speech coach for TED Talk presenters, top political figures, and business leaders describes the action-to-belief phenomenon in the following manner:

> The older, lower part of your brain, the one beneath the cerebral cortex, "thinks" nonverbally. And it thinks faster than your

conscious cerebral cortex. So many of those
things that you do, like hugging your spouse
when you see her at the end of a long day, you
do because you've had an emotional/physical
thought first, and a conscious *"Nice to see you,
honey"* thought only afterward. The body is in
charge, in some significant areas of human
expression.

Taking *action* with your body, in Dr. Morgan's example,
giving your spouse a hug, drives the conscious *belief*,
"Nice to see you, honey." By paying closer attention to our
body language and physically manipulating our bodies
to mimic the behavior we desire, we can help nudge our
brains to align. For example, if my goal is to exude confidence, walking in with my shoulders hunched over or
my eyes cast low will trigger my brain (and others' brains)
to not believe I'm confident. Or when my goal is to stay
open to receiving new ideas, my brain won't accept this
unless my body signals this intention first. So it's important I make a conscious effort to uncross my arms and
legs and loosen tension in my expression.

As much as possible we should take advantage of the
way our self-deception instinct works to drive our beliefs in positive ways. But as helpful as these hacks
might be, we have to remain vigilant. Sometimes, a rose-
colored-glasses view of ourselves royally backfires in a
modern world.

Deception That Derails—Uncovering the Evolved Reasons for Our Lies

Our personal reality is largely what we create, and given that no one is fact-checking our thoughts for accuracy, all it takes is a small shift in our thoughts for our reality to be steered completely off course from the truth. The instinct to present a "best" self to the world sometimes means we do a little photoshop work or apply a filter or two. Who hasn't done a bit of touch-up work on the photos they post to social media? We carefully manicure our narrative, which is not always the most accurate representation, and sometimes this can backfire. That's what happened to journalist Brian Williams.

A beloved NBC news reporter, Williams found himself in the middle of a self-created controversy in 2015 when he claimed that, while covering the Iraq war twelve years earlier, his aircraft had been downed by a grenade. As reports came out that contradicted this retelling, Williams apologized and seemed genuinely confused about how he could have possibly conflated his experience with the experience of those in the aircraft ahead of him—which *had* been downed by a rocket-propelled grenade.

As it turns out, Williams is human and the instinct to self-deceive is universal. Most of us add dramatic elements to our stories and embellish each retelling so as to engage our audience and become the heroes of our own tales. But in a technologically advanced and connected world, such tales will eventually face a reckoning.

As Williams (and nearly every political candidate) has demonstrated, it's easy for us to believe our own lies without questioning the ultimate reason we tell them. In order to not get trapped into our own reputation-shattering tales, it's essential to sort out *why* we are engaging in these behaviors.

Here's a Jewish parable that began as a way of teaching the importance of asking the "why" behind our rituals. I have heard any number of variations and versions of this story, but the takeaway has always remained the same.

> *Sisters Kim, Corey, and Molly all have a holiday tradition of roasting a beautiful turkey every Thanksgiving. They each prepare the turkey the same way: Cut off the ends of the turkey and roast it low and slow in the oven with their mother's special basting sauce. Recently married, Molly is in the kitchen preparing the turkey for her and her new husband's first Thanksgiving together. Her husband is puzzled by Molly's preparation. "Why are you cutting off the ends of that perfectly good turkey?" he asks. "I don't know," Molly responds, "it's just the way we've always done it." But her curiosity is sparked, so she gets her sisters on the phone. Corey and Kim agree, it's just the way Mom always prepared the turkey. They hang up and Molly gives her mother a call, determined to get to the bottom of the mystery: Why, Mom? Why do we cut the ends off the turkey? "Well, now that I think about it that's a good question," Mom replies. "Let me check with your*

grandmother." Molly's mother calls Grandma to finally
get to the bottom of the secret recipe. "Well, I don't know
why you and Molly are cutting the ends off of a perfectly
good turkey," Grandma says. "But I do it because my
roasting pan is too small to fit a whole turkey."

This story perfectly demonstrates the difference between a proximate and ultimate reason for our behaviors.
Proximate reasons are the immediate reason for a particular response; for example, you open your umbrella in the
rain because you don't want to get wet. The ultimate reason is the more distant, underlying cause that is often the
"real" hidden reason driving the behavior (i.e., you don't
want to be wet and catch cold, which could have long-term
effects on your health, or at the very least make your hair
look bad). Molly, her sisters, and their mother all understood their proximate reasons—this was the traditional
way their family had cooked turkey. But none of them had
questioned the ultimate reason for their peculiar behavior
until an outsider drew attention to it.

Most of us believe that when we respond with our
proximate answers we are telling the full and complete
truth. In the case of the roasting pan, the women had
never questioned the why behind the why. In the case of
Brian Williams, his conscious brain was hard at work denying his reasons for lying. His ultimate reason? Brave,
risk-taking men are valued in society. Only Williams
knows for sure, but perhaps he wanted to paint that picture of himself.

So what does all this have to do with you? In order to keep your self-deceptive instincts working for you, and not against you, it's crucial to be conscious and observant of the times when you give *proximate* reasons for your behaviors and desires—*I want to be more like Jeff Bezos because he is rich! He can do what he wants. He owns multiple homes. He drives a Lamborghini*—when ultimate reasons may offer a much more deeply rooted truth. To get to that truth, you must ask the "why" behind the response: *Why do I want to own multiple homes? Why do I want to be rich and drive a Lamborghini?*

Our conscious self actively evades the real reasons our behaviors are driven as they are. The ultimate, instinctual reason men want to be more like Jeff Bezos (or Hugh Heffner or Brad Pitt) is that it affords them status, and status gives them more opportunities to mate. Proximate rewards are nice, but the true prize is driven by our very primal and self-serving subconscious.

Our sex and survival instincts, paired with a healthy dose of self-deceit, lead us to chase after ill-conceived goals (multiple homes and race cars), to promote the wrong people into leadership positions (e.g., tall men with confidence, as you learned in Chapter 2), and to value females for their symmetry as a proxy for their reproductive capabilities. I'm not making the argument that Lamborghinis aren't fun, or that tall, confident men don't make great leaders, or that Miss America winners wouldn't make great mothers. But certainly, leadership and family skills in the modern environment are not inherent to either gender or height, nor are fast cars the true path to happiness. There is some level of deception at play in all of these scenarios.

Women can be especially self-deceptive, for example, about their overall willingness to cooperate with other women. In a meta-analysis of sex differences in cooperation, a 2011 study published in *Psychological Bulletin* found that women are far more cooperative in male-female dyads than in female-female dyads (in fact male-male dyads were more cooperative than female-female pairings!).

Our willingness to be cooperative with men in power is likely an evolved mechanism to secure resources from males who traditionally had value by bolstering their confidence and bending to match their perspectives. But today it perpetuates a vicious cycle whereby women are too cooperative in interactions with male leaders, while unconsciously preventing other women from being regarded with the same esteem. For males, self-deceit might sound like: "I earned this position; my gender and height had no bearing." For females, self-deceit looks more like: "I believe his ideas and leadership skills are stronger than hers; it has nothing to do with gender or favor."

Becoming the Non-Expert

Independent of gender, when people have a vested interest in seeing a situation in a certain light (usually, one that benefits them), they can no longer be objective or clear about how to approach or resolve the problem. Especially when there is an element of embarrassment or status reduction at risk. Our instincts will guide us toward blind trust in our abilities—and maintenance of status— even in light of damning alternative data. Arguably, these are some of the same factors that contributed to the Space Shuttle *Challenger* disaster in 1986.

The *Challenger* explosion is a tragic example of the self-deception instinct gone awry. The contracted engineering company Thiokol had warned NASA that their O-ring products (a critical component to the integrity of the spacecraft) hadn't demonstrated the ability to seal properly in the temperatures that the ship would be exposed to on an unusually cold launch morning. Up to this point, NASA had faced setback after setback and had borne the brunt of express disappointment from the U.S. government on the many previous delays leading up to this launch date. When faced with yet another setback and damage to ego, status, and pride, the team at NASA reacted not with caution at the no-launch recommendation given by Thiokol's engineers, but rather with outright hostility.

Bob Ebeling was one of five Thiokol engineers who had pleaded with NASA to stop the launch. He gave an interview in 2016 to National Public Radio in which it became apparent that he still carried a great deal of guilt in not better arguing his position for the no-launch. But at the end of the day he explained, "NASA ruled the launch. They had their mind set on going up and proving to the world they were right and they knew what they were doing. But they didn't."

The night before the scheduled launch Thiokol executives met privately, for a total of only five minutes. Leaning heavily on proximate reasoning (i.e., pleasing their customer, NASA, and the potential consequence of losing future contracts) they decided to reverse the no-launch recommendation. On the morning of January 26, 1986, seventy-three seconds after liftoff, the *Challenger* exploded in mid-air, killing its entire crew of seven.

NASA hadn't asked what prompted Thiokol's reversal in decision. They heard the answer they needed to hear and were content not to explore deeper. The self-deception instinct cost seven people their lives. The best trained analytical and statistical minds failed to properly evaluate and act according to their own data because said data could be explained away with simple proximate reasoning. No one looked at their ultimate explanations for why they were wanting to push the launch. If they had, they would have come face-to-face with their own need to maintain status. Recognizing the self-deception instinct at work might have prevented one of the most preventable and horrific breakdowns in American history.

When we become the experts, we fight to make our rules correct, often missing the bigger picture of the million points of data we now have access to that could reveal an alternative conclusion. It's easy to fall into old patterns and stories that fit the conclusion we've already decided is correct. But rather than be right, our focus should always be on *getting it right*. *Getting it right*, seeing beyond our innate need to be the expert, is ultimately how we make progress. It's okay to not be the expert in life. Even in fields where we are defined and looked to as experts, we always have opportunity for growth—opportunity to do better.

The reality is that, often, we aren't experts at even the simplest things we are certain we've mastered, even when we think we are. We rely on rules and shortcuts that our brains create in order to move us more quickly to the "correct" conclusion, even when those shortcuts are lies. Only after a disaster occurs do we stop to question, "How did I not see that coming?" Even when things are literally right in front of our faces, our brains are exceptional at ignoring information that doesn't "fit" our truth.

Try the following experiment, which I frequently give to clients and groups. Count the number of F's in the sentence below:

FINISHED FILES ARE THE RESULT
OF YEARS OF SCIENTIFIC STUDY
COMBINED WITH THE EXPERIENCE
OF MANY YEARS OF EXPERTS.

There are, of course, seven. Don't believe me? Go back and count again. Make sure you count the F's that are a part of the word *of*. Would you believe me that four-year-olds are far more effective at this task than adults are? As are nonnative English speakers. Why? Most of the American clients I consult with were taught to read phoneti-cally; as a result, they don't "see" the *f* sound in the word "of" and therefore have a hard time identifying the letter "F" when it's part of that word.

When we lock in on a particular "truth" we lock out anything that contradicts it, actively fighting our con-scious brain. The story, in this case, is that F's sound like *f*. When they don't, such as when they appear in the word "of," we literally can't *see* them. Those who are not yet "experts" at the story—nonnative English speakers or children who haven't yet learned to read—can find the letters without trouble. Often, it takes a non-expert to point out our misconceptions.

The story of Cliff Young encapsulates this idea per-fectly. In 1983, Young, a potato farmer from Beech Forest, Victoria, made an eleven-hour drive to the Westfield Par-ramatta mall. He was not going shopping. The mall was the starting point of the infamously difficult ultramara-thon footrace, spanning 554 miles from Sydney to Melbourne, Australia. Elite racers gathered from around the world, sponsored by big-name shoe brands and run-ning outfitters, to compete in the seven-day event.

When Young arrived in Sydney, he had never entered a marathon before, never trained as a runner, and didn't even own proper gear. In fact, he was wearing overalls and boots. Nevertheless, the sixty-one-year-old farmer was determined that he could complete the grueling event, as he had spent much of his life chasing after sheep on his farm.

No one took him seriously. Especially after the starting gun sounded and Young began shuffling along in his rubber boots with an unconventionally slow stride. But when he crossed the finish line in Melbourne 5 days, 15 hours, and 4 minutes later, Young stunned the world. The old farmer had crushed the world record for the race by nearly a full day and a half!

How did he do it? His advantage was that he had none of the preconceived ideas of elite runners on how to win the race. All the seasoned athletes *knew* that to win they would need to spend eighteen hours a day running and six hours sleeping. While the experts slept, Young kept on running. He didn't even know that he was supposed to sleep during the course of the race. So he didn't. He shuffled along for more than five days.

Sometimes our blind spots can be our breakthroughs. For Cliff Young, his lack of authority in the world of running sent him back to his potato farm with $10,000 in prize money.

Seeking the "Beginner's Mind"

For some companies, recognizing blind spots in their expertise can actually pay off big time. In the early 2000s, a wide body of scientific literature was dedicated to a phenomenon known as the *pharmaceutical productivity crisis*. A much cited 2011 article in the prestigious, peer-reviewed journal *Nature* revealed that while more and more funding had been poured into the development of new drugs, the output of approved products hitting the market had significantly and continuously declined since the mid-1990s.

Pharmaceutical company Eli Lilly had an impressive record of accomplishments, including being the first to produce insulin, first to mass-produce a polio vaccine and penicillin, and the largest manufacturer and distributor of Prozac. But even Eli Lilly was vulnerable to the productivity crisis. Management's first response, even in the face of financial downturn, was to increase research and development, hiring more than seven hundred new scientists in 2000. But if the previous decade had taught the industry anything, it was that more funding, and more of the same kind of thinking, wasn't going to solve the problem. The new hires were stumbling on the same problems and it was time for Eli Lilly to get creative.

Company leadership made a bold move to become non-experts by creating an internet platform for "Seekers" and "Solvers." Rather than only ask *their* research and development team of scientists, why not incentivize *anyone* with a creative solution to a problem? And thus, Innocentive, a crowdsourced problem-solving platform was born. Innocentive became independent of Eli Lilly in 2005, but remains a go-to site for many projects (more than 2,000 challenges at the time of this publication) serving a number of Fortune 500 companies, including General Electric and Kraft Foods. As of February 2020, there were over 390,000 users from nearly 200 countries in Innocentive's problem-solver network, boasting an 85 percent success rate for challenges.

We often erroneously assume that technical problems can only be solved by people with technical expertise, but data from Innocentive have proven this wrong. A recent scientific paper out of MIT Sloan School of Management conducted an analysis of 166 previously unsolved problems on Innocentive from twenty-six firms. Challenges ranged from solutions for synthesizing new chemical compounds to generating a mutant strain of insects resistant to common insecticides and the treatment of inflammation and obesity. Researchers discovered a significant positive correlation between a solution being found and the heterogeneity in the scientific interests of the solvers. In other words, the more diverse the backgrounds of the problem-solvers, the better the odds of finding a solution.

We all know that two heads are better than one, and there is little doubt that 100, 1,000, or even 100,000 differently thinking minds, if well organized, will inevitably drive more creative, profitable solutions.

Eli Lilly, along with many other companies, has benefited from solutions that eluded their highly technical and qualified staff. Nearly 30 percent of solutions came from non-employees and, often, non-experts from entirely unrelated fields. In one such case, toxicology specialists were struggling to understand a pathology that was presenting in their ongoing research. After seeking solutions from both internal and external specialists in their fields, the toxicologists used Innocentive to crowdsource the issue. The solution quickly came from a scientist who specialized in protein crystallography—a branch of science far removed from toxicology. Other winning solutions to the same molecular biology problem have come from an aerospace physicist, a small agribusiness owner, a trans-dermal drug delivery specialist, and an industrial scientist.

Scientific fields aren't the only beneficiaries of crowdsourcing. Kraft Foods recently found itself in need of a new brand identity for one of its most popular products: Oreos. In 2012, Oreo was celebrating a milestone one hundredth birthday and the brand was looking every year of that one hundred. Then Bonin Bough arrived as Oreo's global head of media. Bough didn't have a traditional industry background, which meant he shied away from anchoring the marketing around the same old TV advertisements. He was willing to challenge conventional assumptions. As Bough told *Fast Company* in a 2014 interview, "I asked questions about things that just didn't seem to make sense because I didn't know. I've never had any of that perspective."

The result was a "Daily Twist" campaign that flipped traditional marketing on its head. Oreo crowdsourced its advertising by letting social media channels guide them. Oreo started listening to what people were already talking about online, and then crafted their marketing to fit. If people were talking about the Mars landing, then Oreo's social media ads showed the cookie with Mars-red stuffing and tire tracks running through it. When social media went aflutter over the new Chinese panda baby? Cue the dark Oreo cookie in the shape of a panda face over the cream filling. For Sarah Hofstetter, CEO of Oreo's digital agency, it was a dream campaign: "People were talking about the marketing as much as they were talking about the cookie!" Oreo leveraged social platforms to create an entire ecosystem of PR that, as outlined by a Cannes Lions case study, earned them an additional 4,000 percent–plus Facebook shares (relative to other months), 231 million media impressions, and made Oreo the brand with the highest buzz increase in 2012 (plus-49 percent).

When we are willing to be the non-expert, we often discover surprising solutions to problems we otherwise would never have gotten to—including the problem of knowing ourselves. For example, we cannot see our own blind spots without input from others. Ironically, we are complete "beginners" when it comes to knowing ourselves. Despite the fact that 95 percent of us believe we are self-aware, research by organizational psychologist Tasha Eurich suggests that only 10 percent to 15 percent of us actually are self-aware.

Roger L. Martin, the director of the Martin Prosperity Institute, eloquently explained in a 2010 *Harvard Business Review* article how easy it is to fall into the trap of assessing data with such limited perspective: "By sticking simply to what we can measure," Martin says, "we come to imagine a small and constrained world in which we are prisoners of a 'reality' that is in fact an edifice we've un-knowingly constructed around ourselves." In other words, we can only see through our own eyes, and it's next to im-possible to know what we don't know—especially when the unknown is ourselves.

Achieving self-awareness is no easy feat. How do we know what information to trust when we can't even trust our perceptions of ourselves? I'd argue that we should in-stead turn to the people who know us best and can give us the unvarnished truth. We can crowdsource the solution.

Too frequently, we find ourselves in the position of the elite runners, or the traditional marketers, or the scientists wanting to hire more scientists to solve a problem. We race toward our destinations without ever pausing to check the origins of our own decisions: *Where did that story I'm telling myself come from? Is it really helping me or holding me back? Is it a lie worth telling myself, or am I subconsciously being in-fluenced by my instincts in ways that might not be the most productive or healthy?* Our instinct and need to be *right*, to be the expert, the one with the solution, more often than not, prevents us from moving forward.

One of the best strategies to disrupt the lies we tell our-selves is to adopt the Zen Buddhist principle of *shoshin* or "beginner's mind." The principle encourages us all to adapt childlike curiosity, with an open, eager attitude. If you've ever spent time with a four-year-old you know ex-actly the mindset to which I'm referring. And yes, let's also acknowledge that the constant questioning, *why?* fol-lowed immediately by another *why?* can drive you nuts.

But what if we employed these same curiosity learning principles to our own lives? Try asking yourself three *whys?* for every belief, principle, and excuse—and be brutally honest in your response.

For example, let's say you've gotten into a heated email debate with a colleague about the most productive platform for company communication. You might want to stop and ask yourself: Why do I need to "win" this argument more than I need to solve the actual problem at hand? *Because I am right.* Well, why do I need to be right? *Because I'm not going to let the other person think they are right, when I know they are wrong.* Why do you need them to agree that they are wrong and that your truth is the only truth? *Because then they will respect me.* Why is it important for this person to show you respect right now? And so on. When you dig a little deeper, you can start to see cracks in your instinct and begin to better understand some of the *ultimate* reasons for your behaviors that no longer serve you. Proximate reasons (and justifications) can rarely survive the four-year-old *why* test.

Curiosity and a willingness to rely on non-experts can be particularly difficult for "experts" as we become locked into the constraints of the information and solutions we already know. Zen Master Shunryū Suzuki succinctly explains how the more we know, the more desperately we need to employ shoshin: "In the beginner's mind there are many possibilities, but in the expert's mind, there are few."

Naveen Jain co-chairs the education and global development initiative at the X Prize Foundation, which is committed to crowdsourcing solutions for the world's biggest problems. He believes that experts can only give incremental solutions to problems with which they are too intimately familiar.

"If somebody came up to me and asked how you clean oil in an oil spill, I'm thinking about it very differently from any expert because they know what they have done in the past," Jain told *Fast Company* in a 2012 interview. "So we actually did that at X Prize. We had an oil cleanup prize for $1 million." As it turned out, the $1 million prize-winner's solution was five times better than the method oil company BP spent $20 million on, and was 99 percent efficient. And would you believe that one of the finalists was a team made up of a dentist, a mechanic, and a guy who worked at a tattoo parlor?

We are all experts in our own ways, but that doesn't necessarily mean that the truths we accept are the right truths, or the only truths, or necessarily the best truths, despite what our instincts would have us believe. If experts never engaged in shoshin, if Steve Jobs had never asked why computers shouldn't be carried around in our pockets, or Matt Groening had never wondered why cartoons were only for children, then we'd never have iPhones or *The Simpsons*.

After all, consider how you know anything about anything. Chances are, we can all agree that the world is a sphere, but how do you *know* that? Is it based on what teachers have told you, or what you've seen in NASA's photos from space? Without *direct* personal observation, most of what we know is taken from the shortcuts our brain derives for us (our instincts) or the assumption that what trusted authority figures tell us is true. So in the vast majority of cases, we don't *know* a lot of our own truths, we just trust someone else (or our biology) who might. Quickly this results in an *inattention bias* effect. Inattention bias refers to the way in which we only pay attention to the information that fits our beliefs, while quickly dismissing or justifying away anything that doesn't align with our truths. It's often why people can't communicate across their belief chasms when they can't find ways to see eye to eye.

Yes, and . . . Evoking Empathetic Conversations

In the early 2000s, I was working on a study of crows in collaboration with Cornell's Laboratory of Ornithology. In my role, I fielded a number of questions from the public about one of our most common birds. One of my favorite interactions was when a woman asked me if a crow could be a spirit animal. Caught off guard, I wracked my brain to find the right way to say that, as a scientist, I frankly thought the idea that spirit animals watch over and guide us was ridiculous. I managed to buy some time by simply asking, "Tell me more about that?" I was doing my best to employ shoshin and start from a place of ignorance.

She went on to explain that she'd recently been cross-country skiing in the dead of winter in upstate New York, when she'd fallen and broken her leg badly. She didn't think she was going to make it back home to safety and started to panic. As she told it, that's when a large black crow, her spirit animal, appeared and gave her the mental strength to drag herself home. That crow, she said, watched over her the entire way. It was a heartfelt story. So how was I going to tell this woman that the crow was actually waiting for her to die so it could have dinner?

At that moment, I was given an opportunity to live what I preached: Just because I knew the crow was acting more like a hopeful scavenger than a guide, there wasn't anything to say that my story was necessarily right. I needed to pivot quickly in order to keep my instinct from asserting that my view was the ultimate truth.

"Yes," I said, "a crow can be a spirit animal."

Why? Because I believed her. If she hadn't aligned herself to her truth that this crow was acting as her spirit animal, she likely would not have made it home that day. So sure, a crow might be a spirit animal.

"And..." I continued, "it's also possible that the crow was waiting for you to die so it could eat your soft bits first."

I like to think that I stated my truth a bit more delicately. But that might just be my own self-deception at work.

Adopting the practice of using "Yes, and..." allows for a conversation to continue. This is an especially crucial habit for leaders to develop, whether you run a Fortune 500 company or a five-person team. "Yes, and..." forces you to hear an alternative perspective that might challenge your own reality. Rather than insisting upon your truth, accept that others have truths that they feel are just as valid and real as yours. This is not to say that facts are expendable. It's just accepting that people often have different experiences around facts. For example, someone who is fifty might feel wiser than a twenty-year-old. While it is true that the fifty-year-old does have more experience, that doesn't mean that her younger colleague's different (and potentially valuable) experience should be discounted.

By acknowledging to another that you hear their version with a "Yes, and . . ." you affirm that their expertise is valid. When you meet others where they are—rather than immediately dismissing their viewpoints with a "No!" or even a "Yes, *but* . . ." (which is equivalent to invalidating anything that comes before the "but")—you continue the conversation in a way that might lead you, as the expert, to recognize a new expert perspective. Pursuing *what's* right rather than *who's* right ensures you're reaching the best solution to the problem, rather than appeasing your instinct to be the expert.

As driven by instinct as we are, it's an ongoing challenge to keep from constantly asserting our value and our own positions. But with practice and humility, and by continually rewarding our own and others' inquisitiveness, perhaps we can better tell our own stories. It's my hope that if we challenge our behaviors with the continual refrain of "why?" we may find that the conscious and acceptable answer is: "I don't know."

Chapter 4: Key Takeaways

- Celebrate non-experts (including yourself)
- Challenge the perception of your own rules being the only, or right, or best set
- Explore ways to use the powerful placebo effect for positive changes
- Use actions to drive new beliefs
- Seek crowdsourcing to solve "expert" problems
- Understand not just your proximate reason for a behavior, but the ultimate reason that drives it
- Stop using "but." Try "Yes, and . . ." to carry the conversation forward
- Adapt *shoshin* and ask "why?" a lot

CHAPTER 5

Belonging

Birds of a Feather Crush Competition Together

I**N THE FALL OF 2016,** when Clemson University was headed toward a second National Championship football title, a friend invited me to a tailgate party to watch the Tigers take on their opponents at Memorial Stadium in South Carolina. Football is a sport I'd loved as a kid; I'd spent many summer and fall days playing touch football with the neighborhood boys. So walking to the game that Saturday I felt equipped. I understood the rules. Or at least, the rules on the field.

But when it came to tailgating and pregame rituals, I'd never been exposed to the full-on phenomenon that is Southern college football. The fan frenzy was unlike anything I'd ever seen. Even the attire was more prom-wear than sporting event. In a sea of frilly orange dresses, pearls, and heels, I'd arrived in an old black T-shirt, jeans, and sneakers. I felt like a fool. Why hadn't I been warned? Long before I opened my mouth and my Yankee accent spilled out, it was apparent that I did not belong here. Every single person was wearing Clemson orange. I don't mean splashes in an otherwise balanced palette—this was a full-on color assault: cowboy hats, overalls, bandannas, socks, shoes, body paint. All-in.

Memorial Stadium is one of the largest college football arenas in the country, seating eighty-six thousand fans. As I made my way in, I began to lose my sense of otherness as I picked up on the cadence of the chants: *1,2,3,4,1,2,3,4, C-L-E-M-S-O-N T-I-G-E-R-S fight tigers fight tigers, fight-fight-fight!* I found myself chanting along. Smiling. Blending in with the fans around me. It was electrifying. Hype videos played on a giant board, and we cheered the replays of epic tackles and impossible catches. I was so caught up in the moment, I'd forgotten that I wasn't wearing the right color. My seatmate, knowing this was my first time, excitedly chattered, giving me the play-by-play of the tradition I was about to witness, and pointing out where to focus my attention: the players' entry gate at the top of the hill by the nearest endzone.

Suddenly, the gate parted, and the Clemson team stepped ominously through it, swaying together, arms linked in unity. A cannon sounded and the crowd roared. The entire football team and coaching staff charged down the hill at a full sprint to the roar of a 133-decibel crowd (the loudest audience in college football). Each player paused momentarily as he passed through the gate to rub a ceremonial rock. "Rubbing Howard's Rock became a tradition in 1967," my seatmate explained to me. As the story goes, former Coach Frank Howard used to tell his players: "If you're going to give me 110 percent, you can rub that rock. If you're not, keep your filthy hands off it."

The pageantry and drama were unlike anything I'd ever seen. I loved it. I'd shown up that morning feeling like a stranger, and in a few short hours I had transformed. I was one of the cells of this larger organism, and we were all chanting, moving, experiencing tradition *together*. It was magical.

Clemson knows all too well what evolutionary biologists know: Ritual and traditions wield power. That's why football isn't just a game at Clemson. It's an identity. A brand. A family. A mission behind which every student can stand and feel connected. What Clemson has achieved is nothing short of an extraordinarily powerful instinct intervention. They have capitalized on our very real instinctual need *to belong*.

As social animals, a sense of belonging is inextricably linked to our health, happiness, and workplace performance. A 2019 report by BetterUp Labs, the research arm of coaching firm BetterUp, surveyed over 1,700 employees across a variety of industries: It found that a sense of belonging translated to a 56 percent increase in job performance, a 50 percent decrease in turnover risk, and a 75 percent decrease in employee sick days. Furthermore, the data demonstrated that employees who felt they belonged were 167 percent more likely to positively recommend their place of work. Taken together, *belonging* has a big impact on businesses. Researchers estimate that when organizations facilitate a strong sense of belonging, for every ten thousand employees this benefit could realize:

- An annual gain of over $52 million in productivity boosts
- An annual savings of nearly $10 million in turnover-related costs
- 2,825 fewer sick days being taken during the year, which translates into a productivity gain of nearly $2.5 million per year

When it comes to football, Clemson University has mastered what this data prove: Providing people with a sense of tribe—with a feeling that you are a part of something bigger—is also really good for their bottom line. In 2008, before Clemson built a winning football program, a mere 15,542 freshmen had applied for admission. Ten years and two national titles later, admissions skyrocketed to 28,844, an 86 percent increase. To put that number into perspective, nationwide statistics of comparable post-secondary institutions show a 4 percent *decrease* in enrollment between 2010 and 2017.

In 2017, Clemson played the National Championship game against Alabama. Clemson won the game and 10,800 new social media followers, collecting 27 million total social media impressions for the university. The next week, the university's website was overwhelmed with visitors registering for tours, exploring majors, and downloading application materials. Engineering publicity like that would have been costly and likely less effective. And just as the data from BetterUp Labs suggests, not only did recruitment soar, but 2018 freshman retention increased to 93.3 percent and, as a measure of productivity, the number of total degrees awarded went up 62 percent from 2008.

Our powerful need for belonging also leads us to quickly create *alliances*. The natural ability of our brains to socially categorize humans was studied extensively in the 1970s by social psychologist Henri Tajfel and colleagues. Tajfel uncovered that it only takes ostensibly trivial criteria to produce a strong and biased divide between two groups, something he coined the Minimal Group Paradigm.

For example, we could split a group of twenty individuals into group A and group B with the toss of a coin. Moments later, if we randomly select three individuals from group B to join group A, these migrants would be rated less favorably by the original group A members. Unbelievably, the brain would have already created an us/them, good/bad dichotomy based on nothing more than a flip of a coin. While this may appear discouraging, the fact that our minds can latch on to seemingly arbitrary codes for establishing belonging is actually quite reassuring!

If I'm honest about it, I've consciously used that very circuitry to my advantage on at least one occasion. A few

years after my first Clemson football experience, I was
fund-raising for a charity bicycle ride in support of the Ju-
venile Diabetes Research Foundation. It was a beautiful
fall day and while I was still about $3,000 short of my goal,
I couldn't bring myself to go knock on any more virtual
doors, emailing and campaigning for funds. Instead, I
sought the help of the Clemson fans who had become
"my people." I walked around tailgates, decked out in
Clemson orange gear for about four hours, telling my
football family about my fund-raising mission. They
opened their hearts, their wallets, and, more often than
not, a beer for me. There was an inherent level of trust
granted to me that day based solely on the colors I was
wearing and the team for which I was cheering. I came
home with close to $3,000 in cash toward my charity ride.

How can we establish a sense of belonging and a brand
as well as Clemson does? What would it be like to come to
work every day feeling the connectedness, goodwill, excitement, and belonging that fans feel for their favorite teams?
How can we build *that* level of loyalty and trust in our businesses, our community organizations, and our families?

We first have to understand how strong our instinct
for belonging is—and how it sometimes clashes with our
survival instinct—and then find ways to transform this
instinct for good by creating *cooperative alliances*.

Imagine working in a research team, for example,
where the supervisors are constantly comparing employees' work and pushing them to go harder, faster, smarter.
With no clearly defined tribe, your brain reverts to treat-

ing your colleagues as the "other," an outsider not to be trusted. The entire team will default to fighting and competing with one another, even to the detriment of the company, as a means to survival.

The key to countering this faulty instinct is to create a tribe, an alliance within a safe community. This is precisely what happened to my lab group in graduate school.

Advising Cooperation

In 2009, I had just joined the lab of Dr. Steve Schoech at the University of Memphis. Steve looked and acted like "The Dude" from the cinematic classic *The Big Lebowski*. A high school dropout, truck-driver-turned-revered-scientist, and a researcher who, at the time I'd met him, ran one of the most respected physiology labs in the country, Steve was a genius. Working with him was a dream job.

For six months a year, I lived in Memphis and toiled in Steve's lab; the other six months I lived at Archbold, a biological research station in south-central Florida with about fifteen other students in their twenties from all over the country who had come to work in this unique environment. Our research playground was a five-thousand-acre estate, and my job was essentially to wander around by foot and by ATV searching for *Aphelocoma coerulescens*, or Florida scrub jays, an endangered bird species. Every day felt like I was on the set of *Jurassic Park*. The scenery was stunning; the work was grueling.

When I first joined Steve's lab, I was the new PhD student—meaning I was new competition for attention and grants and, most importantly, birds. When you're researching an endangered species, you're desperate to get every point of data. The only good thing about having a limited number of birds was that we knew every bird in the population as an individual. Each had a unique "name" as designated by lightweight colorful bands that we would place around their legs like bracelets. The biological research station where we worked had two sections: the North Tract, dedicated to ongoing research, with a contingent of year-round interns and staff; and the South Tract, which was essentially "owned" by our lab. We were the rebellious kids who came in for a season and made the southern half our own.

The Schoech lab researchers would go out each day at dawn and scour the South Tract for new birds that we could trap, band, and claim for our own studies. Despite the fact that we were in the same lab, each of us also had independent projects, and we each *needed* those birds for our research. The result was a free-for-all, *Hunger Games*–level competition. We'd spend ten hours in the field, seven days a week, trying to tag as many birds as possible. It was madness; none of us were winning.

Steve rarely came to the field station, as he was tied up with teaching obligations in Memphis. When he did visit, he would sit on the lawn of our field house in his Hawaiian shirt, smoking a stogie and drinking a margarita. Most of us felt like he got in the way. And that just might have been his intention. The more he grumbled about how lousy we were at trapping birds, the more we felt bonded by the experience of having to tolerate him. We stayed up late together, long after Steve had retired for the night, drank his leftover margaritas, and plotted. None of us was about to be out-trapped by this guy.

And then came the day that flipped the switch. Steve had returned from the field that morning with fire in his eyes. Using colorful language that I couldn't possibly do justice, he said he'd just been at the border of the North and South Tracts, where some "snotty-faced intern" from the North had "stolen" one of his birds. *His bird. Our bird. The South Tract Schoech lab's bird!*

That lit a fire under all of us, and was the catalyst for a powerful transformation in our team's behavior. Now, there was an *other*. It wasn't about competing within our own tribe; we were now competing with the North Tract researchers. *They* were the competition. We had been so busy squabbling over our internal numbers, we'd failed to organize against the real enemy. We wanted that bird back. And more.

What transpired was the most innovative year of bird-trapping the lab had ever experienced. We established and organized a new searching system so that each of us would share our birds, allowing us to cover more ground. Our shared spreadsheet was sprawled out across the kitchen table, so we could see where our combined team was searching. We became efficiency machines: tracking, monitoring, entering data, even cooking collaboratively to maximize our time and our ability to advance the mission. We employed new trapping methods, including pulling incubating females right off the nest to mark nestlings. We created highly technical traps that we could bait and close remotely at the push of a button. We even went so far as to develop a radio frequency ID tag to selectively feed *our* birds delicious treats—and not the North Tract "others."

Something else shifted in our lab culture too. We began eating and drinking together. We found time for movies and fun, a little watermelon polo in the local lake, or an impromptu croquet tournament on a Sunday. The entire culture of our lab became more positive. And when it came to capturing birds, we crushed the North Tract. On top of that, each of us enjoyed higher personal returns, scoring more individual birds for each of our projects.

Cooperation, as it turned out, was a far better strategy than internal competition, which had been blinding us to a solution. We had been drawing the boundaries of belonging all wrong. While each of us wanted to gather the most data and appear like the "winner" in the eyes of our adviser, Steve knew that together we could all accomplish more. And he was rewarded as well. Our collaboration led to a significant increase in the number of publications and grant monies coming to Steve's lab.

What happened that summer is the perfect example of how anyone can use one of our strongest instincts, our need to belong, as a way to build positive growth and trust across an entire organization. First, understand that we have a natural tendency to form negative associations with those who are "outsiders" (something we discuss extensively in the next chapter); then, create *positive* associations *within* the team.

I have a slightly embarrassing confession. I travel a lot now, but when I was starting out, traveling for business was a big deal. I remember the first time I was bumped up to board earlier with a small group of passengers. It gave me an immediate sense of importance. After earning more frequent flier miles, I started getting bumped up to first class now and then. Soon, I was eagerly watching the upgrade list on the screen at the gate, hoping for that cleared checkbox beside "R. Heiss." What a thrill when it turned green! I could sit in first class and sip a glass of wine while the others crowded onto the plane behind me. Minutes earlier, I might have been in that second boarding "class," but as soon as I got the upgrade, I felt like I'd deserved it. Like I *was* more important. And when I started getting first-class upgrades before I'd even arrived at the airport, I actually began looking down my nose at the hopefuls at the gate, awaiting their upgrade confirmations. Gosh, just writing about it now makes me feel like a jerk. What absurdity! They were me and I was them on any other flight. I was no better than any other passenger.

The point is: It doesn't take much at all for a company to bolster an employee's or a customer's sense of belonging and the entitled feeling that comes with it. Airline loyalty programs use this ranking system brilliantly, creating a clearly ranked status within the "family" of the particular airline. All the passengers, the family members, belong to the frequent flier club, but it's clear who's earned more miles. The person flying executive platinum has a status-lifting experience, but the privilege isn't limited: Anyone can achieve it. When there is no zero-sum game being played, everyone can win. The achievement of one doesn't have to mean the sacrifice of another.

But now imagine how quickly things can take a turn for the worse if the conditions for status and opportunities to reach that status are limited (e.g., a *very* limited number of seats in first class). Breeding unnecessary competition when there is a finite resource structure almost ensures those feelings of superiority will result in derogatory behaviors, and a culture of backstabbing, ass-kissing, and smear campaigning among those grappling to achieve recognition.

For our ancestors, taking "more" for me and leaving "less" for the others were critical to surviving. After all, it was a scarce and dangerous world, and if you weren't looking out for yourself, no one else was. But in the modern world, cooperative behaviors become the key factor for a team's success. Forgive me for yet another bird analogy, but it's apt: At times, life may seem like a hawkish game of "winner takes all," and we may even think of hawks as majestic hunters with skills we should emulate. But I'd argue to the contrary. We'd fare far better if we follow the strategies of cooperative crows, in life and in business.

Business Is a Game for Hawks
(but Crows Fare Better!)

The much-maligned crow, which I've dedicated a substantial part of my career to studying, is a brilliant bird.
Crows are highly cooperative, choosing to help one
another in extended family groups throughout much
of their lives. For example, when crows forage for food
in a dangerous location, like a road or highway, one
bird will sit out of the feeding activity to play sentinel
and warn the others of potential danger, with a *"Caw!"*
(Or *"Car!"* as the case may be). That's why you've likely
never seen a crow as roadkill. They cover their blind
spots by forming cooperative coalitions to ensure they
maximize their profits (in this case, food) by rotating
responsibilities.

Hawks, on the other hand, are "nature, red in tooth
and claw," to quote Lord Alfred Tennyson. Hawks are
fierce competitors, independent, and ruthless. I've seen
hawks rip young crows directly from their nests to feed
to their hawk young. Some newly hatched hawks even
kill one another in acts of siblicide in a competitive battle
for survival while still in the nest. Hawks represent the
win-at-all-costs mentality that many of us look for in
new hires because we think this person will advance our
business objectives. Being a hawk is seen as a symbol of
strength, power, and competitiveness. But while hawks
may dominate in a single, individual battle, guess what
happens at the organizational level when a company is

composed solely of competitive hawks? It looks like Microsoft in the early 2000s.

At its peak in December 2000, Microsoft was the
world's most valuable company. Just two years later, its
stock had barely budged while Apple's had soared past.
What happened? Microsoft had hired and trained hawks.
It had a policy called "stack ranking," in which co-
workers were ranked along a bell curve, from top
performers to poor performers. Stack ranking turned employees into hawks, competing *against one another*. It
crippled the company's ability to innovate because employee focus was on internal competition rather than
external forces and longer-term market trends. Microsoft
was as disjointed and inefficient as a bunch of young
graduate students desperately grappling for bird data in
the fields of Florida.

A mistake companies frequently make is seeking out
and over-valuing candidates who will do whatever it
takes to get the job done. This kind of mindset can be
amazing when the focus is set correctly—when the "whatever it takes" is to advance the higher mission of the
group. Here, hawks can be valuable when their laserlike
focus is on outside competition. But they can destroy a
group from the inside if they do not become part of the
cooperative culture internally.

Consider what happens when we embrace hawks in
our hiring practices: We rank applicants, hire the "best"
one, throw her or him into the group, and let them be
hawks. Congratulations, you've activated a model of Dar-

winian individual selection—sink or swim/survival of
the fittest—within your company that can prove to be un-
healthy, ruthless, and inefficient.

A fascinating experiment in the egg industry illus-
trates this hawk versus crow divide when it comes to
productivity. Like any good business, the hen-layer industry is always looking to increase its egg production. In an
effort to create a group of super-laying hens, Dr. William
Muir of Purdue University followed the stack-ranking
logic of Microsoft: group the best layers together; leave
the rest behind. Muir selected the most prolifically producing hens, placed them in a coop, and then bred
successive generations from the most productive individual hens. The result? An 89 percent mortality rate of his
poor hens.

The best individual egg-layers were the best because
they were extremely aggressive. When placed together,
they engaged in fatal, cannibalistic pecking, ripping
feathers from one another and viciously attacking bare
skin. Those that didn't die were left with serious physical
injuries. These were hawks in hens' clothing.

Rather than working toward the good of the group,
the super-hens were willing to aggressively suppress
others from being productive. They came out on top by
stepping on others. When hawks are left to rule the roost,
it can be a disastrous outcome for everyone.

Likewise, the traditional hierarchical structure needs
to be destroyed in order to protect cooperative culture at
our places of work. Ranking systems breed internal

competition, driving hawks to focus inwardly to obtain status within the organization. The result looks a lot like hen-pecked birds: Everyone is squabbling to obtain a higher rank; people are willing to trample one another instead of focusing externally on the real competitors.

Cock of the Rock

Establishing rank is something our brains naturally and quickly do because it helps us waste less time and energy fighting about every crumb with each encounter. But it only works under very specific circumstances: when there are clear and consistent criteria for establishing and maintaining rank; and when there's unlimited opportunity for everyone in the "family"/organization to reach the top rank (i.e., no limited seating at the top).

While Microsoft was busy dividing its employees, Apple, its main competitor, had taken the opposite approach. Rather than stack-rank employees, Apple relied on a largely flat organizational structure with a fierce culture of collaboration. The sequential GM assembly line model that brought concept to engineering, to design, to marketing, was dead at Apple. Instead representatives for each department simultaneously worked to create an integrated product.

In a *Business Insider* report on the computer giant, former Apple contractor Brandon Carson explained that, despite Jobs's tyrannical nature, internally the company culture desires and demands a collaborative atmosphere. "Your work is peer-vetted," he said. "We had to present our work to the team and take feedback." Another unnamed source told *Business Insider*, "The general idea is this: You are part of something much bigger than you. The ideas you talk about in the hall, the neat tricks you figured out in CSS [cascading style sheets], the new unibody machining technique, that's part of your job, something you are paid to do for Apple's success, not something you need to blog about to satisfy your ego. Don't f— it up for everyone."

Apple capitalized on the strong human instinct to belong. It kept teams small and sworn to secrecy (hence the unnamed source above). The competition employees faced weren't for rank or title. Rather, they were challenged to make the organization as a whole better. They were all trying to fly first class.

Apple also did something extraordinary that shines a light on another important point about our tribal instincts: Sometimes as leaders, we have to be willing to step into the role of the common enemy in order to draw a team closer together. We have to play hawk. At Apple, rather than the combativeness happening between workers, it came from their captain.

Steve Jobs was infamous for his temper tantrums and impatience. He would harshly challenge employees of all ranks, at any time, about whether they had what it took to work at Apple. Debi Coleman, an original member of the Mac team, told *Harvard Business Review* that "[Jobs] would shout at a meeting, 'You asshole, you never do anything right.'" And yet, according to Coleman, she and everyone else on that team considered themselves the luckiest people on the planet to be working for Jobs. He was willing to be the enemy because consciously or not, he knew that his intolerance of anything less than perfection pushed his team of players together. His goal was to create a company that was run by ideas, not by hierarchy. Only the best ideas were acceptable, and in order to get those best ideas delivered it took a full team of A players, or very talented crows, coordinating their skills.

This technique is precisely the approach that my adviser Steve employed in his lab, and Clemson's Coach Howard applied on the field, when he told players: "If you're not going to give me 110 percent, keep your filthy hands off my rock!"

Sometimes having a hawk at the top can work. But as others who have tried to emulate the tough styles of these leaders often find, knowing *when* to play hawk and when to switch tactics is essential. I can relate to the terror a lot of Apple employees felt around Jobs. I certainly always wanted to be on my A game around my own adviser. But I'll also never forget that during my oral exams for my doctoral degree, Steve stood up to one of the other committee members who was grilling me with absurd and irrelevant questions. Steve said to him, "If you're through being an asshole, I think we're done here." My loyalty was forever secured to Steve Schoech from that moment forward. While he may have been a hawk in most interactions, when an outside threat came knocking, he was the first to have my back and turn that hooked bill outward.

Good Game (Theory)

Most of the decisions we make are driven by fear or reciprocity—which is, arguably, rooted in fear at some level as well. For example, reciprocity might only work because we fear the potential consequences of failing to reciprocate. "I'll scratch your back if you scratch mine" is a powerful driver of cooperative behaviors. When we observe crows (the actual bird), we see that they are willing to "sacrifice" feeding time for the good of the group. Crows have figured out that the "sacrifice" of time away from eating (i.e., a good back scratch) comes with a huge return: They can gorge more efficiently later.

The calculus that makes this work is a mathematical model called *game theory*, which crows use to their full advantage. Game theory models how consciously thinking individuals *should* behave in a given situation to maximize their own personal benefit. The benefits could be something tangible, like a raise or more vacation time; or they may be more abstract, like power, happiness, or achieving the attention of a lover.

Let's imagine how game theory might play out in a workplace setting if we have a culture of hawks, who are all competing and willing to do whatever it takes to advance their individual positions. It's helpful to have a visual representation of a "payoff" for which individuals would be competing, so let's use arbitrary numbers as a demonstration of benefits, and say that 5 points is the potential payout for a win. If, in any given interaction, a person within the group behaves "hawkishly" toward another (for example, stabbing a colleague in the back to get a promotion), that will benefit the hawk while hurting the colleague who behaves more "crowlike," or cooperatively. The standings for hawks and crows within the company thus far:

HAWK = +5
CROW = 0

But what happens when the crow, angered by this interaction, decides to act hawkish? In the next encounter, they both behave as hawks, denigrating one another to the deficit of all. Now, they may ultimately split the 5-point resource, but there's also a cost to both because they sustain injuries (physical or reputational) due to their fighting. Their efforts to outdo one another have only prevented forward progress on projects and ultimately made both of them look bad in front of their group. The "payoff" is now closer to:

Hawk 1 = +2.5 (split resource) − 3 (cost of fighting)
= −0.5 (overall reward)
Hawk 2 = +2.5 (split resource) − 3 (cost of fighting)
= −0.5 (overall reward)

Even if a hawk does win some share of the resource for which it is fighting, the cost of fighting and the continuous negativity that it generates will inevitably land the hawk in a net-negative situation.

So what would happen if instead of pursuing an individualized hawklike strategy within a group, people all behaved more like crows toward one another? This type of thinking relies upon purposefully generating a strong sense of belonging in the group. The more anyone feels like they belong, the lower the temptation is for anyone to behave like a hawk.

Individually, the initial payoff may not look so appealing to all the hawks out there:

Crow 1 = 2.5
Crow 2 = 2.5

The crows will evenly split the resources with no fighting cost associated.

But why accept portions when a full 5-point resource is available? And why would any individual cooperate with another when the payoff looks to be less? The trick is to zoom out to see the potential payoff on a different level of competition.

It's not that the crows are rolling over and playing dead when they cooperate internally. They are simply saving their fight for the *right* competitors. It seems counterintuitive, just as sitting sentinel while the rest of the crows feed doesn't initially seem like a good strategy. And yet, by actively engaging in reciprocity, the overall returns are far greater. The temptation to be a winner-take-all hawk may drive us toward quick-fix solutions, but it only gets us relatively ahead of our internal competitors. (That is, if there is an "ahead" to achieve.)

Let's imagine a few fictitious teams in a start-up company. Team A is filled with crows, all behaving cooperatively to advance exciting, new projects together, independent of individual compensation or credit. As a whole, their overall team score is 2.5. No great individual gains, no great individual losses. To be clear, this scenario does not preclude rank. Certainly some crows will be entitled to larger or smaller shares, but ultimately, the resource is still divided cooperatively, without challenge. Everyone understands his or her own level of contribution.

Now imagine team B, a mixture of crows and hawks, and team C, which is exclusively hawks, all behaving competitively and trying to get a leg up on one another. Projects in teams B and C likely progress in fits and starts, as leaders emerge by stomping on the shoulders of those they are competing against in order to appear better (this might look like taking credit for ideas, or denigrating friends to look more appealing to potential mates). The *overall* team scores will be closer to −0.5. Some individuals are making gains, but others are taking losses, and all are fighting over a zero-sum set of resources in rank, recognition, positioning, and titles. In other words, there are "fighting" or "competition" costs associated with each reward. These teams cannot emerge unscathed or unscarred.

If team A (all crows) and either team B (mix) or C (all hawks) compete directly, who wins? I hope it's obvious to you by now that the answer is team A.

This is true in business and in the wild. Watch for it next time you see a group of crows antagonizing a lone hawk in the air. When actual crows are gathered in groups, all calling and carrying on, it's often because they are working *together* to drive off a hawk. Likewise, in our imaginary start-up, neither teams B nor C stand a chance. Put one hundred hawks against one hundred crows, and the crows will systematically, in a coordinated effort, drive off each hawk by acting together as a much larger bird of prey, while the hawks are all too busy being concerned with their own needs and fighting over who gets to eat first. The technical term for a group of crows is a *murder*. This is no happy accident.

At the group level—in biology, business, and life—cooperation wins. When employees and teams of any variety understand the power of cooperation, and how to use competition most effectively, they can collaborate to crush competitors and dominate the market. This is when the rewards begin to roll in, in the form of new contracts, raises, and bonuses. When the group does well, so do all of its individuals. That initial smaller payoff we invest at the group level now comes in tenfold at the individual level.

Getting What You Give

Crows demonstrate for us the concept of *reciprocity renewal*—the gift that keeps giving. Reciprocity renewal is
the recognition that giving something away doesn't always mean we have less. In fact, reciprocity works
because it is *renewed*. It's not a pie that can only be
sliced so many ways with each slice becoming smaller.
Rather, when a selfless leader empowers those around
her, she will find she has *more* power. Her team will
function more efficiently and reinforce her position of
leadership. Clever experiments in the lab of Dr. David
DeSteno at Northeastern University have even demonstrated that when subjects feel grateful, they are 25
percent more generous in their exchange of economic
goods, which in turn makes others grateful, creating a
positive feedback loop that greatly benefits all that are
a part of the group.

More for others doesn't have to mean less for us in an
environment of abundance. So many things—power,
money, love—that our instincts would have us believe
are finite simply are not. Quite the opposite. They can be
renewable resources, used to build relationships of reciprocity among cooperative crows, ensuring they will be
renewed again and again.

Our biology *already* wires us to want to reciprocate:
When someone does something for you, you feel a debt
is owed. Using this natural biological mechanism, you

can build a daily practice around building reciprocity. Once a day, go out of your way to "sacrifice" your time, your money, or—perhaps the most powerful—your attention. It doesn't have to be a major commitment. Maybe it's simply stopping on the street to help out that stranger who looks like they might need directions. But here's where things get tricky: You can't *expect* anything in return.

Our brains release dopamine in *expectation* of a reward. When it doesn't come, those dopamine levels crash, leaving us feeling pained. Think back to the last time you had high expectations for a promotion at work or a birthday gift you were certain your significant other had purchased for you. When that promotion went to someone else, or the present wasn't what you'd expected, you felt deeply disappointed.

Instead, when we train our brains to *not expect* a reward, then if the reward comes, *surprise* reciprocity gives us an even *bigger* dopamine hit than what we would have felt if we'd anticipated the promotion or the special gift.

There's another incentive to retraining our hawk instincts to expect a reward: Turns out that when we do something kind for another, that act in and of itself gives us a rewarding hit of dopamine. Research finds that the act of giving makes us feel happier and increases the chances of us doing kind acts again in the near future. Thus, the positive feedback loop is reinforced and kept going by our own *internal* gauge of happiness, rather than relying on the unreliable return from others (which may or may not come).

By taking thirty seconds out of your day to reflect and physically contribute positively to the world in some small way, you begin to retrain the resource-scarcity mindset of your brain, the part of your brain that compels you to behave like a hawk. Rather than ruminating on what the world owes you, you start to see how your actions contribute positively to your own mood and to your community. Instead of feeling the disappointment of expectations not met or gifts not yet received, you experience true pleasure when those unanticipated rewards come back to you. You start to recognize that the most valuable things in life, like cooperation, love, belonging, and purpose, are renewable resources. The adage "you get what you give" proves itself time and time again.

Social media tycoon, entrepreneur, and Wine Library CEO Gary Vaynerchuk recounts in his blog about a time he delivered a single, low-cost bottle of wine to a family in the middle of a snowstorm. It was a costly decision, but his reward, as Vaynerchuk describes it, was the dopamine-rich feeling that he delivered the highest customer service above and beyond expectation. And then, a secondary unexpected hit came: The customer's son was so delighted with the service to his family that he called a few weeks later and placed a huge order with the company. Doing the right thing comes with its own reward, but sometimes unexpected secondary reciprocations can further the positive cycle.

Cultivating a Crow Culture

Building membership among your many tribes and teams of cooperative, reciprocal groups can grow those groups exponentially, not only in physical wealth but in more intangible riches—like a sense of community, cooperation, belonging, and loyalty.

A wide body of research indicates that strong social connections are the key to a better, more productive life. And that can begin with a common and basic trust that if I do for you, so shall you return the favor for me. Harvard researchers have been tracking the health and happiness of 268 sophomores in a longitudinal study that first started in 1938. The major finding so far? People with good relationships have more overall happiness and health than people with poor social connections. No other factor was more influential. Not money. Not fame, or number of vacation homes, or amount of candy bars you can eat in one sitting.

The secret to well-being has never been the excess accumulation of resources (homes, race cars, sexual partners), but rather, well-being comes with cooperative reciprocity. In other words, happiness can be found in a community of like-minded crows.

Biologically, our dopamine system actually rewards us for engaging in cooperative reciprocity. When given the option to give to charity or keep the money for ourselves, the same pleasure areas of our brain will light up under both circumstances, indicating that giving genuinely makes us feel good. In fact, at least one study published in *Science* reported that those who spent money on themselves were less happy than those who spent money on others. In an abundant world, study after study confirms that it feels good to give, cooperate, and lend support to others.

Building a culture of belonging takes time and trust. But given that we are naturally inclined to follow the rule of reciprocity, we should use this to our advantage to nudge our and others' instinct toward these positive feelings of belonging. The more reciprocity we elicit, the more we believe in, trust, and cooperate with the group around us.

One way to build trust and cooperation is to create family-like bonds among your co-workers, teammates, neighbors, and friends. Why is it that so many successful leaders talk to employees as if they are all a big family, all working toward a single goal? Perhaps they know that we are hardwired to trust our families.

In family groups, a high degree of relatedness means that if you cheat and steal from your brother, genetically you are also cheating yourself. Because siblings and parents are related by about 50 percent, whatever you take from your sibling or parent you are also taking away from 50 percent of *you*. From a strictly genetic perspective, when they lose, so, too, do you. Equally, their wins are shared by you. It might seem like an altruistic act when a brother gives up a position so his younger sibling gets the promotion instead. But the brother that loses out on the promotion is getting some benefit via his relatedness to the promoted sibling. In other words, when you're re-lated to the winner, you, too, are winning.

Businesses looking to promote cooperation and al-truistic contribution among employees would be wise to create family-like atmospheres. One of the simplest ways is to establish a common set of traditions in which every-one can choose to participate: once-a-month bowling night, Friendsgiving dinners at the office in February (be-cause why not?!), social media viral video attempts, nature hikes, and more.

At Archbold Biological Station we established Mon-day night "family dinners," with the cooking and cleaning responsibilities rotated through the entire crew. Not only was the variety of meals delicious and different, we often would stay after all the cleanup had been done, talking, swapping stories and songs, and playing instruments long into the night.

Sometimes even silly traditions help employees feel like they are all sharing an inside joke. Plasticard-Lock-tech International hosts a "Gag Awards" night, giving away trophies and awards for the goofiest things that hap-pened throughout the year. At consulting company Human Dynamics, at 3 p.m. everyone spins in their chair for thirty seconds to get people laughing and refreshed from the afternoon slump. In one of my favorite ongoing traditions, Ruby Receptionists, a company out of Port-land, Oregon, celebrates Fridays by dressing up according to a chosen theme. They have sported everything from special hats to costumes dedicated to memes.

This dynamic works among a wide variety of groups: Pajama day at school, crazy hat day with the bowling league, and neighborhood block parties all serve the same purpose. It matters little what the traditions of your own organization or family become, so long as everyone feels accepted, invited, and able to participate. The boundaries here can be a bit of a tightrope to walk: No one wants to feel forced to participate, so it's important that traditions be encouraged, but still evolve organically. But building a sense of camaraderie in good times will pay off and sustain your tribe through tough times.

To get the most of employees, they need to feel truly vested in the organization itself. This is perhaps why employee-owned companies tend to be so successful. Research done by the National Center for Employee Ownership demonstrates that employee-owned companies perform better and have significantly lower turnover than their counterparts.

Southwest Airlines, which is roughly 13 percent employee owned, understands how important a sense of family is, especially when times get tough. Its annual traditions include doling out millions of dollars every year on March 15 as part of its profit-sharing plan. A strong emphasis on a family culture is what Southwest credits for its survival during the significant reduction in passenger airline travel following 9/11. During the massive downturn, many airlines laid off employees. But Southwest didn't let a single employee go. Instead co-founder Herb Kelleher asked the team to share a general pay cut to help save the employment of their brothers and sisters. Amazingly, they still managed to make money in the fourth quarter of 2001. Just as they suffered together, they celebrated with a $179 million contribution to the employee profit-sharing plan delivered, as promised, on time.

Leaders can break hawkish behavior and spur reciprocity and cooperation by being willing to model crowlike behaviors first. LinkedIn's CEO Jeff Winder did exactly that when the company stock plummeted in 2016. Rather than cash in on his $14 million stock bonus, he turned the money over to employees, boosting morale and belonging within the company long enough for stock prices to rebound to nearly their original value.

Sometimes a crisis, when framed appropriately, can build bonds between colleagues such that they *feel* more like family and are willing to invest in one another to the benefit of everyone. During the COVID-19 crisis, companies around the world had an opportunity to come together to save jobs. Amid the major revenue declines in publishing, *Buzzfeed* cut pay for nearly every employee, and CEO Jonah Peretti declined to take a salary. Other organizations from all different industries followed suit. Chuck Robbins, CEO of technology conglomerate Cisco Systems, said in an interview to *Bloomberg*: "We're actively involved in the community trying to help people who've been impacted by this, why would we contribute to the problem?" Various concessions, from pay cuts to furloughs, were made by nearly every company that suffered during the COVID-19 pandemic. Everyone was trying to stay afloat and keep their employees on board the ship as well.

Without a clear sense of belonging it would be easy for companies in any crisis to have their employees turn to hawks, desperately scrambling to get what they all individually could, leading to the ultimate demise of the organization and unemployment of its employees.

Breaking (out of) Bad

Being vulnerable and generous affords others the opportunity to reciprocate and break out of the cycle of hawkish behavior. In 1980, Robert Axelrod, a professor at the University of Michigan, solicited game theorists to compete by submitting strategies that were either cooperative (crow) or selfish (hawk) in various contexts. As each strategy was run against the others, patterns quickly emerged. Axelrod determined that one of the most destructive patterns occurs when a crow is *misinterpreted* in an interaction as a hawk. In this case, the other player turns hawkish as a defense. The original player in turn behaves like a hawk—even though she's a crow—and so the pattern of hawkish, destructive behaviors continue to the detriment of both players.

We often find ourselves locked in similar patterns at work and in our lives: One person perceives a wrong and, instead of forgiving or confronting the other about the problem, we instead adjust our own behaviors to *match* the indiscretion. This locks us into the same destructive patterns. I recently spoke to an intimate group of twenty CEOs in Ohio. As I began challenging some of their beliefs, I watched one man lean back from the table he was sitting at, cross his arms, and furrow his brow. In workshop settings like this, I ask participants to actively challenge and generate discussion of the ideas that I'm presenting them. Judging from his body language, I knew I was about to do verbal battle.

Sure enough, he opened fire on me, pushing back against some of the ideas I had just presented. My instincts took over, and I charged back at him. It went on like this for most of the presentation, with the discussion growing more intensely heated—and personal. I distinctly remember watching him during breaks and thinking less than gracious thoughts about his moral character. I actively avoided being around him, and watched him do the same with me, both of us snubbing the other in subtle but poignant ways.

Near the end of the day, I gave the group an exercise in which everyone had to speak one truth from the workshop aloud. As we went around the room, each person participated in turn with overwhelming positive feedback. And then it came time for this man to speak.

"You know, for most of the day I didn't much like you," he said. That was it. I pride myself on not needing to be "liked" by others, so long as I am bringing them value, but this comment struck a nerve. It was off topic.

An unnecessary insult. I steeled myself with a vengeful comeback to launch at him. Thankfully, before the words could slip past my lips, I recognized a shift. His posture had changed. He had sat back down at the table, and leaned in. Where there had been a frown I caught the slightest upturn of his lips. My response caught in my throat as he continued speaking.

"I was wrong. I was defensive and angry by what you were saying and fired that anger at you because it was easier than looking at my own behaviors," he said. I felt my heart drop through my stomach. I hadn't given this man credit for any of his astute commentary all day, because I had been so charged up to battle him at every interaction. I had failed to lead the group as well as I could have, because after my first interaction with this man, I dismissed any further contributions he had made to the discussion as either frivolous or insulting. But as soon as he softened, I felt my defenses break down too. As I went to leave for the day we embraced through tears and thanked one another for the lessons we both were able to glean from the other.

Being vulnerable is challenging. No one wants to be perceived as weak or allow someone else to take advantage of them. But as research professor and best-selling author Brené Brown so eloquently observes, "Vulnerability is not winning or losing; it's having the courage to show up and be seen when we have no control over the outcome. Vulnerability is not weakness; it's our greatest measure of courage." How can we be more vulnerable within our communities while maintaining the strength we need to defend ourselves from the occasional hawk? I think we need to take a closer look at how we define our boundaries of belonging.

Finding a Common Enemy

I would love to tell you that our brains are wonderfully harmonic, peaceful places. But the reality is, they are not. Our brains are constantly redrawing enemy lines, typically arranged around familiarity and a willingness to grant favor. While these lines were once useful in determining the real enemies beyond our tribal group, in our modern environment of flimsy boundaries this instinct can quickly turn into unnecessary squabbles between colleagues and co-workers, or between departments, missing the bigger picture—that we are all working toward achieving the same thing.

However, we can use this instinct to our advantage.

To counter the negative aspects of our tribal instinct, we must *consciously* establish strong new "enemy" lines. Don't draw them based on familiarity or temporary favor— but rather draw enemy lines that can clearly stand up to internal challenges. Consider the lines we draw around sports teams: You and I might disagree on who should be pitching, or whether they should have attempted that field goal, but ultimately, we are still cheering for the same outcome: We want our team—our tribe—to win.

I am a huge Boston Red Sox fan. Walking into Fenway
Park, I know my tribe when I see them. They are all
dressed in the right colors, wearing the right logos, and
cheering for the right team. I drink with them, high-five,
and even sometimes hug complete strangers because of
their red socks. Of course, I can still instantly judge and
mark my enemy: those New York Yankees hat–wearing
losers. I sling my venomous hatred of those Yankee fans,
obviously, with a good bit of humor. But anyone who fol-
lows sports knows that nothing beats a good rivalry game.
That's because there are clear enemies on either side.
And nothing draws an in-group together more than a
clear and common enemy.

Several major corporations have figured out this powerful way to define belonging and are successfully using
it to their advantages. Think about who the common
enemy is in each of the following organizations:

   Coke
   McDonald's
   Mac

Pretty easy to come up with Pepsi, Burger King, and
just about any PC-maker, right? When organizations can
quickly and clearly define a common enemy—a competitor outside of their own company—it taps into an instinct
that would otherwise send our brains to draw enemy
lines around whole departments or challenge another's
good ideas or single out the "others" on our team.

Still, we have to be careful when we devise a common-enemy competitor. What happens if a rival suddenly becomes a member of your team? (Recall the members of Tajfel's Minimum Group Paradigm studies who faced discrimination after moving into a new group, despite having been randomly assigned to groups at the start.) It's difficult to overcome the negative associations and affiliations you've assigned them.

Instead of choosing a physical "other" to demonize, it's better to make the enemy more abstract. Rather than seeing all things PC as a common enemy, Mac turned toward the abstract: poor design, clunky, boring, conventional thinking. These became the common enemy, launching an era of colorful iMacs, iPods, iPhones—and a cult following among those who believed in the slogan "Think different."

There's a common-enemy story I like to tell about a maintenance worker at a hospital. One day, he was fixing a swinging door when a stranger walked up and asked the man, "What are you doing?" The worker could have given a range of responses: "I'm fixing the door"; "I do whatever my boss tells me to do"; or even "Why do you care?"

Instead, he said: "At this hospital, we believe in making every effort to minimize the pain of the patient. When our patients are being wheeled through this area, this door sticks and jars them in their beds, causing them discomfort. So, I'm helping our patients be more comfortable; I'm simply minimizing patient pain."

This response captures the essence of an organization that has *fully* executed a perfect instinct intervention. This

hospital created a strong, abstract common enemy: patient pain. How powerful will your organization be when
the equivalent of your maintenance workers, surgeons,
nurses, and anesthesiologists are all sharing a common
enemy? Who will your common enemy be? With the will-
ful and thoughtful creation of an outside common enemy,
you can generate a powerfully united in-group.

Surrounding ourselves with people who push us to be
our best by giving us theirs is healthy for everyone. From
football to research teams to the corporate office, *we are
all stronger together.*

Chapter 5: Key Takeaways

- Use Minimal Group Paradigm to help establish
  positive alliances throughout your organization.
- Remember that "winning" doesn't mean some-
  one else has to lose. This isn't a zero sum game.
- Create family-like atmospheres by establishing
  traditions.
- Focus externally on a common enemy.
- Be vulnerable enough to admit you may have
  been wrong.
- Establish a sense of family with reciprocal re-
  newal.
- Model crowlike behaviors.

CHAPTER 6

Fear of the Other

Why Strangers Still Signal Danger

FOR MANY YEARS, I'VE HAD an image embedded in my brain of one of my first experiences at Archbold Biological Station, a 5,200-acre research institute near Lake Placid, Florida. One day, I saw a tall man dressed in protective gear, standing in the middle of the Florida sand pine scrub, a critically endangered habitat that's home to nineteen federally listed endangered species. Suspended in his left hand was the drip-torch he had just used to set fire to dozens of acres of this precious resource.

To anyone outside of the tribe of biologists who understand fire ecology, this man would have seemed like an absolute terror. A beast. A threat. When we don't understand a look, a culture, a behavior, our first instinct is to villainize. That's our "fear of the other" instinct on full display. Yet despite all appearances, this man wasn't destroying the ecosystem—he was saving it. I learned that his name was Shane Pruett, and he was a post-doctoral student and trained volunteer who took part in the prescribed burns that are vital to better land management for this unique habitat.

Lightning-strike fires occurred regularly throughout Florida's history. But as humans settled into the land, habitats fragmented. The habitat-protecting fires were quickly squelched to prevent destruction of homes and farms. Soon, the very *absence* of regular fires would threaten the viability of Florida's scrubland diversity. Today, only about 10 percent of Florida scrub remains. Sometimes, even with the very best intentions, we eliminate or mismanage vitally important elements in our environments. In the case of the sand pine scrub, a lack of fire nearly spelled extinction.

Our communities and places of work have an uncanny way of reflecting nature's lessons when it comes to the intricate way diverse elements are needed to maintain and better a system.

Business Imitates Biology

There isn't a company or leader today who needs to be convinced about the importance of diversity. Reports from McKinsey & Company (2018), *Harvard Business Re-*

view (2013), and leadership performance company Clover-pop (2017), respectively, have found that more diverse companies are:

- 35 percent more likely to have higher financial returns
- 70 percent more likely to capture new markets
- 87 percent better at making smart decisions

A 2020 report from Citigroup demonstrated that the U.S. economy as a whole had lost about $16 trillion over the course of twenty years by not correcting inequities in access to small business loans, higher education, and housing credits for the Black community.

But even with all this evidence, and more supportive research that rolls in regularly, our tangible progress toward a diverse workforce still remains stalled. According to a Deloitte 2018 census, white men dominated leadership board chair positions (91 percent), while white women and minority men comprised a measly 4.3 percent and 4.1 percent, respectively. Minority women made up a pathetic 0.4 percent. The *New York Times* reported in 2018 that there were more CEOs of Fortune 500 companies named John than there were women CEOs by any name. It wasn't until 2018 that any Fortune 500 company had an openly gay woman serving as CEO.

And even as American corporations promise to increase diversity on their boards, a *New York Times* 2020 analysis found that "the boards of the 3,000 largest publicly traded companies remain overwhelmingly white." In fact, of the 20,000+ directors they analyzed, Black directors made up just 4 percent of all boards and Black women made up only 1.5 percent. I would argue that shifting these underwhelming numbers begins with a better understanding of some basic biological principles.

Nature has a natural order to community development that is remarkably similar to how our businesses operate and organize. As a result, the organic formation of diversity in nature and diversity in our organizations closely mimic one another. The way ecological communities grow, develop, and change is referred to in biology as *succession*. In business and in nature, our communities are continually changing and being disrupted by outside influences, competitors, and shifting priorities. Nothing remains static, but the degree to which an environment is affected by disruption is worth consideration.

Biological succession naturally operates on cycles. A disturbance, like a fire in the Florida scrub, disrupts and refreshes the stages. Sticking with fire as an example, the burn will clear out a lot of the species that were beginning to dominate the landscape, giving a chance for those seeds that remain dormant in the soil to germinate and have a fighting chance to get the nutrients they need to thrive. Without a disruption, whatever opportunistic species that takes hold in the landscape first will dominate, quickly establishing and outcompeting other organisms. In biology, this most populous and present organism is referred to as a *dominant species*.

You've likely heard of a coniferous forest (spruces/firs) or maybe even taken a walk through a deciduous forest (maple/oaks) in the autumn. We reference these ecosystems by their dominant species because it's the most noted characteristic of the landscape. You wouldn't likely hear anyone talking about the moss, or ferns, or shrubs, or fungus, or weeds—all of which are also very present in these landscapes—but not dominant.

Once a dominant species emerges, it is the biological "end" to nature's succession plan. In other words, it's very difficult for a new species to gain traction and impossible to overtake the dominant species without a disruption. The environment can creep toward a monoculture, as the nutrients are soaked up by the dominant species, and the landscape becomes exceedingly difficult for any other species to survive. The others are literally shaded or crowded out—at least until a disturbance begins the cycle again, like Shane Pruett did with his drip-torch.

What does all this mean for our organizations? If we want to keep ideas fresh, resources flowing, and have the ability to quickly adapt and flourish in a rapidly changing environment, we need to establish multicultural landscapes that promote diversity. And we need to start by taking that drip-torch to our own instincts—our own dominant way of thinking.

Based on our dreadful workplace-diversity statistics, most business environments could easily be classified by their dominant markers: white males. As such, diversity would be crowded out by the established "flora" that is better at obtaining resources (in the natural world this would be things like sunlight and nutrients; in the corporate world this might be interviews, promotions, equal pay, and network introductions) simply for the fact that they have been there longer (not to mention any number of human cultural factors that come into play).

It's critical to note that the dominant species is not necessarily acting with malice, or intentionally being exclusive, or that the other species are less qualified to flourish. Even non-dominant species in the natural ecosystem are likely to take aim at the new tender sapling over the hardened bark of an established tree.

But a lack of understanding of the biological drivers that can be hacked to foster more diverse ecosystems, in my view, is at the *core* of why our diversity and inclusion programs continually fail. We are neglecting to address the underlying elements of our biology. It's imperative that we explore these biologically established norms, stories, shortcuts, and instincts that drive us. When it comes to diversity, the core tenet rooted in the very soil of nearly every ecosystem is an instinct to fear "the other."

The Trouble with a Tribe of 8 Billion

It seems absurd that in a globally functioning world in which the average cell phone user has 308 contacts and 338 friends on Facebook, we are still spooked by people who are different from us. A 2016 Pew poll on Race in America found that 75 percent of white Americans discuss important matters among a network of people who are entirely white, with no minority presence. A similar story unfolds among Black Americans, of whom 65 percent report that their networks are composed entirely of other Black people. When it comes to *feeling* safe, we naturally move toward people we recognize as part of our tribe, our dominant "species" (despite the fact that at the genetic level, there is no measurable discrepancy between races).

In fact, our brains evolved to feel comfortable around no more than 100 to 150 individuals who look alike, think alike, and operate under the same cultural norms as us. This number of people, sometimes referred to as Dunbar's number, is calculated as a correlation between the size of a primate's social group and the size of its neocortex, the part of the brain that processes sensory, motor, language, emotional, and associative information. It represents the approximate capacity of the number of stable relationships we are capable of maintaining, given our brain size. This range was the best number of people for knowing each person individually, as well as how each of those people relate to one another.

For our ancestors, anyone who fell outside of a stable set of contacts likely wasn't a friendly neighbor dropping by to borrow a cup of sugar. Strangers, and in particular people who looked different, elicited a full-on stress response as our bodies primed us for safety: *This un-*

known other might be here to battle me for my limited supply of food and sexual partners. Our bodies prepared us with increased stress hormones because it was better to be wary and safe.

The same *Minimal Group Paradigm* that allows us to identify and find a sense of belonging can also work to separate us from others. To make sense of the world, our brain quickly categorizes people into groups, often based on external characteristics like race or gender. It assigns an associated story to that person based on their similarities or differences to us, for example: safe/unsafe, good/bad, positive/negative. Given that our ancestral groups were often in conflict with other groups, it was evolutionarily advantageous for our brains to develop key shortcuts to keep us safe, a formula that looks like this:

People similar to us = Good
People different from us = Bad.

Obviously, we are now way outside the norm of knowing just 100 to 150 people. With the power of a device that fits in our hand, we can instantly connect with just about any human being on the planet. Yet our instinct to fear the other persists.

Our modern brains still draw boundaries around what we deem to be the "norm" (i.e., those who are like us). And our poor bodies are still responding with an elevated stress response whenever someone who looks different walks into the room. (Consider how it must feel to the person walking into a room full of strangers who don't look like him or her!)

Even as we become a more global society, the strength of our associations have not wavered much, leading us to treat unfairly those who are not like "us." With genetic pools mixing, cultures in continuous flux, and accessibility to digital and physical travel allowing for the exchange of ideas, we should be acting like one giant, 8-billion-person tribe. But our brains are not built for this world—and it is costing us dearly.

Case in point: In April 2018, two Black men walked into a Starbucks in Philadelphia to wait for a third man with whom they had a scheduled meeting. The men asked to use the bathroom, but were told it was only for paying customers and they had not purchased anything yet. When they sat down at a table, the manager, who was white, called police and the men were arrested on suspicion of trespassing. Amid the social uproar and widespread criticism, Starbucks made a formal apology, and then closed eight thousand of its American-based stores for an afternoon of racial-bias training. The company lost approximately $12 million from the closures, not including a hard financial hit in reputation. Would the outcome have been different if the manager of the store was Black? Would the police have been called if it were two white customers waiting to start a meeting without having purchased anything? What about a group of moms? The key driver here is fear.

Fear of the other extends beyond the color of our skin. In two separate incidents in 2015, Southwest attendants did not allow certain passengers to board flights because other passengers complained about them. Why? Because they feared they were Muslim. In another instance, passengers were actually removed from Southwest flights because they were "acting suspiciously" by changing seats and speaking in Arabic. In fact, one of the passengers, *Khairuldeen Makhzoomi*, was an Iraqi refugee and American citizen studying political science at UC Berkeley. As he tearfully told the *New York Times*: "I couldn't handle it and my eyes began to water . . . the way they searched me, the dogs, the officers. People were watching me and the humiliation made me so afraid because it brought all of these memories back." *Makhzoomi*'s father had been a diplomat before he was abducted, imprisoned, and murdered by Saddam Hussein. *He* had every right to be fearful. His fellow passengers? Not so much. But when we rely on our instincts, fear of the other causes us to react without thinking, missing important context.

Our fear instinct has also been allowed to run amok on technology platforms. Black passengers using ride-sharing apps such as Uber and Lyft experience double the number of cancellation rates and 35 percent longer wait times than white passengers. A study at Harvard shows that on Airbnb, renters with African American–sounding names were 16 percent less likely to be accepted by hosts compared to renters with white-sounding names. These sorts of highly offensive reactions have to be readjusted for our modern world. We can't let our fear of the other instinct override our better judgment.

Why Sticking to Our Own Won't Work

In my advisory work, I occasionally hear unsettling sentiments such as, "Perhaps we'd all be better off if we were to simply stick with our own kind." Or "Why not just let everyone return to their respective corners and just interact with those who are similar to themselves?" (It may sound shocking to some, but these are verbatim quotes from advisory calls.) Such isolationist policies have historically led countries into dramatic decline as we lose valuable collaboration and technological advancements that a diverse citizenry brings.

When we actively choose to avoid or ignore diversity in our own companies and communities because of the discomfort it might bring, we are actively limiting ourselves from our best outcomes. As we explore several examples of this, keep in mind a key lesson from biology: *Bio-diversity breeds stability.* Every introductory biology student can tell you this ecological law. It's a fundamental truth of nature and it holds across quotidian life as well.

Consider the Irish potato famine as a cautionary tale. Farming in Ireland in 1845 essentially involved planting a monoculture, or one crop: potatoes. Potatoes are typically a sturdy crop, but that year a virulent disease destroyed the leaves and edible roots of potato plants, turning them black and rotten. Monoculture led to the starvation deaths of a million people, and a million more were forced to emigrate from the island.

A less-deadly, though still important, equivalent to this in modern life is when you make decisions from a monoculture of thought patterns—when everyone in your life and your boardroom is a potato. Don't get me wrong, we need potatoes! But we need to intentionally plant other crops if we don't want a single perspective to dominate, which could starve us of novel ideas and innovations.

A monoculture at work can even lead to embarrassing and potentially disastrous mistakes. When Honda was getting ready to introduce its new economy-car model the Fitta in Sweden, it had a cute tagline: "Small on the outside, big on the inside." Sounds good, except *fitta* in Swedish is a vulgar word for vagina. Clearly, not a single Swedish speaker had been consulted on what to name this model. Luckily, someone caught the translation blunder before the vehicle was launched and the name was changed to Jazz.

Diversity isn't just good for a company's public reputation; there are proven benefits to being around those who think differently than you. A study from the Kellogg School of Management found that heterogenetic groups (those composed of individuals from a variety of races, ages, genders, and socioeconomic backgrounds) were significantly more engaged, creative, and accurate when solving a problem than homogeneous groups. Their willingness to challenge one another and bring new

perspectives and backgrounds to the problem were ultimately what allowed them to best solve the challenges at
hand. When we fight our instinct to fear the other, we
avoid putting our company at risk of that single devastating blight capable of decimating our company culture.

Tailwinds

Our misplaced biases show up constantly with new technologies. I recently watched viral videos on Facebook that
showed white men and Black men in a public restroom,
attempting to wash their hands. The white man puts his
hand under an automatic soap dispenser and a squirt of
soap drops down into it. Then a Black man tries it. Nothing. In one video, the Black man grabs a white paper
towel and uses it on top of his hand to activate the dispenser. It works perfectly. The technology in these
dispensers emit soap when a hand reflects light back to
a sensor. But light is absorbed by dark skin, rather than
reflected. As such, the technology fails completely for
dark-skinned individuals. Did the companies that design
these flawed dispensers think to test them outside of
their immediate group? Any diversity in the testing pool
would have led to someone recognizing and flagging the
problem before it was too late.

I call these kinds of circumstances "tailwinds"—and
they occur when we are so blind to our own privilege that
we don't notice the friction and frustration that others,

with a different set of privileges, might experience in the same situation. As a cyclist, I will never forget my first one-hundred-mile race. I had trained and put in countless hours. But who's ever really ready for a seven-hour day in a bicycle seat? At the fifty-mile turnaround point, I was surprised at how good I felt. I'd anticipated that the race would be *a lot* harder. But I was barely breathing heavy. And then, just as I pushed off to head back to the finish line, I had a startling realization: There was a strong wind in my face. I hadn't even noticed that it had been blowing at my back the entire time. Now, it was gusting hard against my every press forward. My return trip took nearly double the time. I was miserable for most of the last fifty miles.

In my misery, this experience got me thinking about privilege. It's very easy to accept our experience as "normal." When there's a tailwind at your back, you simply don't feel how easy things are for you. When the world is designed for you, and for your lighter skin, you don't often notice because things just work the way they always have.

Let me give you a very simple construct to help you stand in another's shoes for a moment. Imagine that you're one of the 10 percent of Americans who are left-hand dominant. Here's a very small sampling of what's *not* made for you, does not consider your unique difference, and can be a constant source of frustration:

- School desks
- Scissors

- Power saws
- Cameras
- Kitchen knives
- Computer setups (with mouse)
- Firearms
- Golf clubs
- String instruments
- Video game controllers

If you are left-hand dominant, then you understand headwinds. You've probably recognized how all of these things annoy you or complicate your life. But the right-hand-dominant folks barely notice. They're riding the tailwinds.

Unnoticed tailwinds can be extraordinarily costly to business, but to be clear: Ensuring diversity isn't just a means to avoiding potential loss and embarrassment. There are huge *opportunities* when we consider new perspectives. Take the case of the Band-Aid, invented and marketed as a "flesh-colored" bandage in 1920. Let that sink in for a minute. For over a hundred years, Johnson & Johnson has made bandages to match the skin of white people, leaving a massive amount of market share on the table (not to mention, exhibiting total disregard for the needs of its nonwhite customer base. Only in June of 2020, amid widespread unrest over racial inequity in America after the murder of George Floyd, did Johnson & Johnson announce it would begin production of multi-skin-toned bandages—a move that likely comes too late. Tru-Colour,

a bandage company launched in 2014, had already cap-
tured the loyalty of many people of different skin tones
whose physical and societal wounds had been too long left
ignored. (And, in strictly business measures, Tru-Colour
was faster to recognize value in the $1.3 trillion annual
buying power of African Americans and the $1.7 trillion
driven by Latinos—both, rapidly growing markets.)

Eliminating Bias in Hiring

Our instinct to fear the other can squelch opportunities
to grow and cause us to miss fresh talent. Think about
your business. Who makes the majority of the decisions?
Are there enough stories being heard and perspectives
being considered, or are you at risk of a metaphorical
famine? It is an evolutionary desire to surround ourselves with people we feel most comfortable with. But the
far better action is to expand our in-groups and nudge
our instincts away from a stranger-danger impulse, especially when they creep into our hiring practices.

In 2003, scientists sent identical résumés in response
to help wanted ads found in Boston and Chicago news-
papers. Some résumés bore examples of traditionally
Black-sounding names—like Lakisha and Jamal—
whereas others were submitted with white-sounding
names, like Emily or Greg. Strikingly, even though the
content of the résumés was the same, those with pre-
sumed white names received 50 percent more calls for

the same position. These findings are perhaps less shocking when combined with data from the Bureau of Labor
Statistics showing that the number of Black individuals
holding management positions (presumably, people who
might be conducting the hiring) was 50 percent less than
the number of white managers.

It's really important to pause here and drive home the
point that this instinct doesn't make us bad people. It
makes us human, with brains that are built to keep us
safe. By and large, we are blissfully unaware of how much
our instincts drive our behaviors. But this is by no means
a justification. It's our responsibility to do better. And we
can do better in our hiring practices by using some of the
same tools introduced in Chapter 2, for example, following the example of companies like GapJumpers, which
remove biasing information from résumés and ensure
we aren't only excited about candidates that look like us.

Spending Time with "Others"

Close your eyes and take an imaginary walk down your
hallway at home. Take a look at the pictures on your walls.
Look at the photos on your refrigerator, by your bedside.
What do you see? Now pick up a magazine in your living
room and flip through the pages. Or think about the last
movie or TV show you watched. Most of us, whether it's
in the faces looking back at us in our photographs or in
the media we consume, find reflections of ourselves.

One of the simplest ways we can intervene in a fear-driven instinct is to spend more time around people who are different from us. Science backs this up. The mere exposure to a set of faces, whether similar to or different from ours, increases our fondness for them. A 2008 study out of Brandeis University found that continued, increased exposure to faces from a different race enabled participants' brains to expand the generalization of that race *category* to be "likable" beyond just the familiar individual faces. Then, even when participants were shown novel faces from the race category with which they'd become familiar, participants increased their likability ratings of those faces.

The interactions don't even have to be personal. Another study from the University of Wisconsin–Madison found that exposure to different cultures through television is enough to intervene in our misguided instinct. Participants were assigned to watch either *Little Mosque on the Prairie*, a Canadian sitcom about a Muslim family, or *Friends*, an American sitcom with no references to Muslim culture. Participants assigned to *Little Mosque* showed a significant reduction in anti-Muslim attitudes even six weeks after they'd finished watching, while those who had watched *Friends* showed no change in attitude. Other studies from the University of Minnesota have used television programs with positively depicted prominent gay characters (NBC's *Will & Grace* and HBO's *Six Feet Under*) to demonstrate a reduction in anti-gay prejudice post viewing.

I can personally testify to how powerful exposure to others is when assessing likability. I grew up in a small town in upstate New York—and I mean *small*. The kids you met on the playground at age five would likely be the peers that surrounded you all through elementary, middle, and high school unless they, or you, moved towns. With a graduating class of about one hundred people, you knew everyone and everyone knew you. This had its charms. But as a teenager, I couldn't wait to escape!

Social media platforms were beginning to take root, and I remember having a MySpace account late in high school, but then we all moved over to Facebook by the time I entered college. As a result, I stayed in contact with nearly all of my graduating class. For all the homogeneity of a small, white, upstate New York class, we were spread wide across the political and ideological spectrums. During the divisive election of 2016, I was horrified by the behaviors and opinions of some of my classmates on social media, often thinking to myself: *No way is he voting like that! Does she really think that way? How?*

My classmates had developed deeply disparate ideologies. But what strikes me now as particularly fascinating about this time was my own behavior. I gave passes to people who behaved abhorrently online simply because I *knew* them. I excused hateful rhetoric and engaged in conversations and debates with these "friends" simply because we had shared experiences. Had I heard the same commentary from a stranger, I would have immediately dismissed and disengaged.

But here's the lesson: The power of familiarity can work both positively and negatively. Here is an opportunity for us to practice the intervention of "yes, and . . ." in which we step into the truth of the other. Instead of immediately dismissing the other person's perspective, take the opportunity to build empathy, then carry the conversation forward from their perspective before adding your own. It may seem easier to engage in cancel culture and public shaming of voices that dissent from our own, but it's far more rewarding and effective if we work to better understand the truths of multiple perspectives. Perhaps your truth, your experience, isn't the *only* one—but the only way you'll ever know is if you don't immediately shun anyone outside of your circle. The more we shut out and separate dissenting voices the more radicalized we become in our own circles, setting up a dangerous precedent. Instead, we can embrace and engage people who are different from us in "yes, and . . ." communication, building empathy with virtually zero effort.

This can be especially effective when the people who are different from us are actually already in our circles. In the small town where I grew up, I knew a number of people who held negative opinions about the LGBTQ community. When my friend, a beloved member of this same small community, came out as a lesbian, people were forced to confront two conflicting "truths" they held:

1. Amy is a wonderful person and

2. LGBTQ people are sick, immoral, or otherwise dangerous threats to family and society.

Once she was out, their logic to support both truths could no longer hold. They had to choose: Either this individual that they had known and adored for any number of reasons over the years was suddenly no longer wonderful, or all people that identified as LGBTQ weren't abhorrent threats to society. Most recognized the truth that needed shifting. After all, my friend hadn't magically transformed into something evil. The community knew her as an *individual* first. Her sexuality didn't fundamentally change the person she was and is. For some, the thought process went like this:

1. Amy isn't terrible, therefore
2. I guess people who identify as LGBTQ aren't fundamentally bad people.

Some might call it hypocrisy. I call it learned empathy.

Famously, Nancy Reagan, a staunch conservative, took a progressive stance on stem cell research when she recognized the benefits for her beloved husband, President Ronald Reagan, who, at the time, was succumbing to Alzheimer's. The more we can actively surround ourselves with others who hold dissenting opinions from our own, the more chance we have of better understanding not just our own truth, but a larger universal truth that bends and shifts and arcs differently for everyone.

That's not to say that some don't hold abhorrent opinions, but it's worth pausing first to acknowledge and recognize their perspective with as much empathy as possible. What if we are actually the ones holding the abhorrent opinion. How would we want to be embraced, challenged, and accepted?

President Obama often talked about the "empathy deficit" that fuels misunderstandings and conflict. "There's a lot of talk in this country about the federal deficit. But I think we should talk more about our empathy deficit," he once told a Xavier University graduating class in a commencement speech. "The ability to put ourselves in someone else's shoes; to see the world through the eyes of those who are different from us—the child who's hungry, the steelworker who's been laid off, the family who lost the entire life they built together when the storm came to town. Learning to stand in somebody else's shoes, to see through their eyes, that's how peace begins."

Whether we are working toward global peace, or simply the daily practice of reducing conflict between team members in our office or family members at dinner, empathy is an important skill to cultivate. It's an effective intervention in our fear instinct.

In what has to be near the top of my list of all-time fun experiments, a 2015 team of scientists tested the reactions of students to painful stimuli as they submerged their hands in ice-cold water under different test conditions. Subjects were assigned to either endure the ice activity alone, or together with a friend who also submerged their hands, or with a stranger, or with a stranger after both were dosed with metyrapone, a drug that blocks the stress hormone cortisol. After each trial, students were then asked to rate their level of pain. Subjects who were paired with a friend suffered the most, suggesting that their empathy for a friend's pain raised their own pain levels. Fascinatingly, participants who were given metyrapone also showed increased empathy for the stranger. But subjects paired with strangers, with no stress-blocking drugs, had pain reactions that were not significantly different from their pain reactions when they were alone.

But here's the best part of the experiment: A final condition was tested in which the researchers paired two strangers and had them spend fifteen minutes together playing the video game *Rock Band* before dunking their hands in ice. These strangers reported more empathy and concern for one another than the strangers in the first two conditions, simply because they had been teamed in a cooperative and fun environment for a mere quarter hour. This shows that in order to increase empathy among teams or pairs, all it takes is making a little music! As lead researcher Jeffrey Mogil noted to *Science Daily*, "It turns out that even a shared experience that is as superficial as playing a video game together can move people from the 'stranger zone' to the 'friend zone' and generate meaningful levels of empathy. This research demonstrates that basic strategies to reduce social stress could start to move us from an empathy deficit to a surplus."

When we are willing to play games with the "other," we can capitalize on surprising rewards, like better problem-solving. Researcher Katherine W. Phillips's group at Northwestern University had participants play detectives in teams to identify suspects in a murder scenario. Her results demonstrated that homogeneous groups were more confident in their decisions, even though they were more often *wrong* in their conclusions than a diverse group's members, who felt *less* confident despite being more accurate than the homogeneous group. Confirmation bias and squelching of new ideas in the homogeneous groups produced a false, feel-good, "we are all in this together" perspective (as you'll recall from Chapter 5, it's the danger of the instinct to belong). *Being* right was more important than what *was* right. The comfort of a conforming in-group must be sacrificed if we are to move forward in our quest of seeking truth from a diversity of perspectives and interpretations. But make no mistake about it—this is hard work.

Flexing Discomfort

Our brains need to be worked, just like any other muscles in our bodies. You wouldn't run a marathon without first training to run a mile. And yet, every day, we are asking our brains to perform at an elite level of comfort around strangers. In the best of circumstances, this stranger-exposure training is uncomfortable for us. But it is only in this discomfort that our brains grow stronger, we become more in charge of our responses, and our instincts get to take a backseat.

When athletes train, they actually produce microscopic tears in the muscle fibers of whatever muscle they're working. It's not a comfortable process, and frequently this training can cause some pain—a feeling we may fear and largely seek to avoid. But just as the weight lifter pushes herself through an uncomfortable workout to grow her muscles, you, too, require some hardship and exertion to allow your brain and relationships with "the other" to grow. Exposing our brains to new ideas, new perspectives, and the challenges brought on by the discomfort it creates allows us to do some heavy lifting. And it's in this space that we get to rewire our brains' outdated "truths" about the other.

It may help to consider how our brains like to operate. Our brains tend to think in a binary fashion: Either you are safe and comfortable or *you're going to die!* Even dipping a toe into the space of discomfort—going alone to a party, giving a speech at your best friend's wedding, meeting your partner's parents—can feel to your brain like a very real threat.

One of the best, and most counterintuitive, interventions that can help to quell an over-stressed modern brain is to *proactively seek discomfort* at work, at home, and in our social lives. Safe and healthy forms only,

please! What's key is to desensitize your brain to the nerv-
ousness we all have around others, leaning toward,
rather than away from, that feeling.

Essentially, you're going to parse out the things that
deserve your stress response from things that don't. In
the process, you rewrite the story your brain has been
telling you, which no longer serves you in the modern
environment.

There are so many creative ways to seek out discomfort, and it's not even necessary for you to directly interact
with someone different from you in order for this exercise
to work. You simply need to elicit the same generalized
stress response that we all get whenever we're feeling nervous. For example, you could strike up a conversation with
someone whom you've never spoken to before; send a
thank-you note to a colleague who's not expecting it; sign
up for the volleyball tournament even though you've
never played; write a poem to share publicly; vow to tell
the truth for twenty-four hours; say "no" to an assignment
you otherwise would have passively accepted.

My personal favorite discomfort challenge? Go find a
room to be by yourself, shut the door, crank your favorite
tunes—and *dance*. I'm not talking about two-stepping
and snapping your fingers. I mean *really* get after it. You'll
hear a little voice in your head saying something like,
"Wow, my hips don't move like that." That's your chance
to rewrite your subconscious story. *Sure they do!* My hips
move however I say they do, because I get to control this
story. Once you get too comfortable, invite a friend over.

If that doesn't make you squeamish, post a video of it on YouTube. And send me the link so I can share it on my Fear(less) Blog at www.rebeccaheiss.com!

The point is to rewire the part of your brain that believes discomfort = death. By actively seeking it out—by being told no, enduring embarrassment, and, of course, by occasionally dealing with people who aren't exactly like you—you're training your brain to recognize that these situations aren't plunging you headlong into an actual dangerous situation.

When you give your brain a chance to ruminate on the action (*Was this conversation really what I was so worried about?*) and weigh the outcome (*Hey, I'm still alive!*), you can start to distinguish between stressful situations that warrant a fight-or-flight response and those that amount to nothing more than a bit of embarrassment— or maybe even some new dance moves!

Soon enough, when discomfort arrives in the form of a stranger who doesn't look like you walking through the door, you've already trained your brain to recognize the reaction your body is having. You can respond without fear, panic, or the risk of offloading important decisions to a stressed-out, survival-obsessed brain.

When you step outside your comfort zone, you become more open to the fact that *your* race, gender, political ideology, religion, and more might not be the *only* or *best* option. This can be an incredibly uncomfortable yet profound awakening. Not only might "the other" not be so scary, they might very well bring the solution that changes the landscape of your organization for the better.

Chapter 6: Key Takeaways

- Be willing to be the fire or disruptor. Challenge ideas and rules that have taken root in your organization.
- Seek opportunities to eliminate barriers for the non-dominant "species" of your organization. How can everyone have equal voices and access to resources?
- Be willing to engage in the difficult conversations. Ask others to assume positive intent on your behalf and assume positive intent of others.
- Check your tailwinds. How might others be experiencing an event differently than you?
- Proactively seek opportunities to spend time with those who are different from you.
- Use bias elimination tools to remove unconscious bias from your hiring practices.
- Get comfortable with discomfort with fear(less) challenges.

CHAPTER 7

Information Gathering

Staying Curious in the Clutter

N OT LONG AGO, I SAT on a beautiful beach watching my beloved splash about in the waves while I rested contentedly on the shores shoveling a burger into my mouth. "Come on, come in," he prodded me, "the water is amazing!" *Nope*, I shook my head and took another giant bite of burger. *I'm not going in there,* I thought. *There might be a shark!*

Now, the lack of logic of this response does not escape me. I already knew, for instance, that there are, on average, only two fatal unprovoked shark deaths *globally* each year. And I was aware that over half a million Americans die each year from heart disease—something I certainly was stacking my odds in favor of as I scarfed down that burger "safely" on the sandy beach. Yet even in the face of facts, I was operating on instinct instead. We all do this. Because despite having access to unprecedented amounts of data, we still have trouble making sense of it all.

Our instinct for data collection has earned us the label "informavores" by psychologist George Miller. We crave information the same way we desire junk food, drugs, and sex. A 2019 neural imaging study out of UC Berkeley's Haas School of Business found that the same neural pathways light up whether we are introducing cocaine or simply acquiring new information. Both trigger rewarding hits of dopamine. And we get that reward even if the information we acquire doesn't help us. "To the brain, information is its own reward, above and beyond whether it's useful," says Ming Hsu, one of the study's co-authors. "And just as our brains like empty calories from junk food, they can overvalue information that makes us feel good but may not be useful."

Knowledge collection was undoubtedly an important evolutionary adaptation for our ancestors. Having access to more relevant information about where food might be, or that Melissa in the cave next door has access to warm layers, would have helped us make better decisions and increase our chances to survive (e.g., be extra nice to Melissa as the days get colder!). In collecting information, our brains believe we are mitigating risks that might lead to bad decisions. And by having all the information possible before making a decision we are, generally, in a better position to make the right choice.

Unfortunately, our drive for knowledge consumption is wildly mismatched with the current expansive data landscape. According to the International Data Corporation (IDC), the digital universe will reach 175 zettabytes in 2025. For those of us who don't speak the language of data, a single zettabyte is equivalent to the approximate number of observable stars in our universe. I still struggle to put that into perspective. Data solutions platform NodeGraph attempted to quantify this by tallying up a sampling of all the data in 2020 that we globally processed in one minute, of a single day, on the internet. That data included: 200 million emails sent, 4.2 million Google searches, 4.7 million YouTube videos viewed, and 480,000 tweets constructed. All in sixty seconds of time. With this dazzling display of information all my brain can come up with is the imagery of a cartoon character's eyes reading *"Tilt!"*

Despite the fact that our brains can't keep up, we are determined (and rewarded by our own dopamine system) for trying. So how does a brain built to seek information function when there is data overload? The answer is: poorly.

The trouble is threefold:

1. **POOR DATA COLLECTION:** We have far more data than will ever be useful. Our brains evolved to be data-gathering machines, taking in as much input as we could manage, which might have been fine in the more sparse, immediate-

return environment of our ancestors. But just as our digestive tracts are overwhelmed by the amount of food we have access to in the modern environment, so, too, are our brains becoming obese with junk information. With the excessive amount of data at our fingertips, we feel increasingly overwhelmed and stressed. Survival instinct fully engaged, we search for reassurance, a quick fix, a clear explanation of all the unknowns out there. Unfortunately, we can almost always find those data. The data may not be correct, but we greedily consume it to squash our fear of the unknown, often reinforcing beliefs that may or may not be accurate.

2. **POOR DATA ANALYSIS:** We are lousy at interpreting our data. Having cherry-picked or been fed specific types of data, we then correlate meaningless points together to tell a story that may or may not be an accurate perception of reality. But the interpretation *will* help to justify the decision we've already made or the position we have already supported. Our brains process information in terms of relationships and associations. The interpretation of the data doesn't have to be correct in order for the story to stick.

3. **POOR DATA APPLICATION:** We collect, analyze, and apply data to serve only our own purpose. Rather than starting with an agreed upon question that requires any and all answers, we begin

with an answer and then find the data that can
be interpreted to justify our story. And with the
overload of data currently available to us, there
is no shortage of ways we can poorly apply it.

Let's do a deeper dive on how our information-
gathering instinct exacerbates these three issues in a
modern world.

Poor Data Collection

A research study from Experian Data found that 88 percent of all American companies are still relying on "bad
data" that directly impacts the bottom line. Bad data
come in many forms, but it generally refers to information that is erroneous, misleading, or missing as a result
of poor collection techniques.

A 2018 Gartner Research report found "the average financial impact of poor data quality on organizations is
$9.7 million per year." IBM cites a higher, $3.1 trillion annual loss for American companies. Ironically, even the
data on the financial impact of bad data offer such a
broad range that these numbers, too, are left wildly open
to interpretation.

With the nearly infinite number of sources for collecting information, it becomes too easy for us to add more
data, increase our sample size, and become bogged down
in our own information-collection loop. The result is a lot

of irrelevant junk data that muck up any insights that may have been useful.

In an interview for *Harvard Business Review*, former General Electric CEO Jack Welch once said: "Insecure managers create complexity. Frightened, nervous managers use thick, convoluted planning books and busy slides filled with everything they've known since childhood. *Real leaders don't need clutter.*" Yet our days are filled with clutter from constant personal and professional data input: dinging phones, health trackers, six different social media platforms with their attendant engagement reports, news blasts, and so on. We are collecting countless pieces of information at unprecedented rates, keeping us locked in a cycle of *chasing* data, rather than *driving* it. And when we allow data to be in the driver's seat it's easy to lose sight of what we were originally chasing.

Finding an answer to every question is certainly appealing and would have been evolutionary adaptive. But in the modern environment of information overload, finding clear, unambiguous answers is next to impossible—unless, that is, you choose to do exactly that.

A multitude of studies have found that social media use, in particular, biases us toward data that already align with our views, reinforcing polarized opinions and increasing our propensity to dismiss contradictory information. We adapt the first data that we see that makes sense based on our current position, then we collect more data to support our side. When I was a professor, I watched my students unknowingly engage in this behavior frequently when they were doing research using search engines. Rather than type in the question they were trying to answer, they would query the position they were looking to support. For example, when I would challenge my students to answer the question "Are vaccines dangerous?" they would begin their search query with "vaccines are dangerous" or "vaccines are not dangerous," and only collect the data from those queries.

In terms of simplifying data, a filter of black/white, correct/incorrect, truth/fiction, news/fake news makes everything significantly easier to cope with. Once we adhere to one camp, we only have to pay attention to the data that validate that position. But only seeing one position by gathering data from only one perspective leaves us further from the truth than we began.

A story about Tesco, a grocery retail with over thirty-five hundred stores in the UK alone, helps to demonstrate the disasters that might unfold when we only seek data to prove our position. Tesco actually owes much of its success to being one of the earliest adopters of big-data. Tesco tracked customer activity and used targeted advertising by studying shoppers' habits with loyalty cards. In 2010, twenty years after Tesco began analyzing card data, they accomplished a sevenfold increase in profits. An impressive feat! But then the company became complacent. It began collecting and valuing the wrong kind of data, missing the bigger picture of their clients' needs and, ultimately, took a hit to their bottom line.

To understand how Tesco's fortunes took a turn, go back to 1995. That's when Tesco announced a state-of-the-art marketing scheme in the form of a customer loyalty card. The "Clubcard" gave shoppers more incentive to spend because they received points for every purchase—points that could be exchanged for vouchers to spend in store on items they regularly purchased or at other partner organizations. To enroll in the club, customers had to provide a few personal details such as home address, telephone number, and dietary preferences. Then, any time they made a purchase, they presented their Clubcard to earn points. In exchange, Tesco scooped up excruciatingly detailed data in the form of shopping preferences, purchases, and patterns. As Edwina Dunn, CEO of Dunnhumby, data analysts for Tesco, told the *Guardian* in 2003, "You can find people interested in cooking from scratch, or people who shop with distinct flavours in mind, or where convenience is key. We are trying to track lifestyles in terms of what is in the basket." Tesco also generated personalized online and offline discounts based on a customer's data, collecting even *more* data when customers used those discounts.

Tesco's data-gathering system was a huge success—at first. Just one year after the Clubcard was introduced, members spent 28 percent more at Tesco and 16 percent less at their main competitors' stores. In addition, Tesco began collecting commercial income in the form of payments from suppliers every time their promotions were put in front of consumers.

But by 2013, the shine began to wear off. Tesco's beloved data demonstrated that customers were weary of their habits being tracked, and had grown tired of gimmicks and coupons. They were switching to discount stores that didn't track their data, such as Aldi and Lidl. A survey of over eleven thousand consumers in the UK—conducted by watchdog group Which?—rated Tesco the worst supermarket, citing poor customer service and steep pricing.

As its profits fell, Tesco ramped up promotions, tried to raise more revenue through its suppliers and commercial income, and made a desperate attempt to analyze its way back into the hearts of its customers. Yet they overlooked one major detail: the data that pointed to what customers actually wanted—less tracking and lower prices.

Sometimes Tesco missed the mark in major ways. In a case described by University College London associate professor Hannah Fry on OneZero, a Tesco customer said she was shocked to discover condoms on her online "favorites" shopping list. Insisting that her husband never used them, she complained to the analysts that the data they were getting from her loyalty card must be faulty. The analysts issued an apology, but the data weren't corrupt. Her husband had been buying condoms. He just wasn't using them at home! Even grocery lists can be deeply personal.

In 2015, Tesco posted a $9.6 billion loss and its stock plummeted. In an interview with the BBC during this tumultuous time, the former CEO of Tesco, Sir Terry Leahy,

described the company as having failed to maintain customer trust. "What [customers] really needed were lower
prices and they needed a price list that they could trust,"
he said.

Tesco delivered the opposite. It was so determined to
prove its data were good, Tesco forgot why the company
was collecting information to begin with—to better serve
customers. Tesco got swept up in chasing data money
trails and manipulating its customers, rather than serving them.

Luckily for Tesco, new management and a new direction helped the retail giant to refocus its values back to
shoppers and a 2019 data marker showed customer satisfaction was the highest it had been for years.

Whether it's a multi-billion-dollar company, a small
hometown business, or a curious individual seeking answers, when we fail to pause and first *think* about how
best to collect data we risk massive consequences.

We are often tempted to believe that more information can only lead to better, more customized results (a
dangerous combination of our variety and information-
seeking instincts). But our data-gathering instinct may
lead us down a dangerous path because we are wired to
tune in closely to *immediate* data—especially as that data
apply to people. Data cues were once vital for us to recognize and maintain our own standing in our ancestral
tribes: *Who is hanging around? What are they consuming?
Who is leading? Who is providing resources? What resources
are being valued by others?* And on and on. Collecting this

kind of information helped us fill in any signals we may have missed. But when we apply these instincts to a digital world in which the granularity of the data is constantly increasing—such that we are measuring, daily, hourly, or even to the minute how we are showing up in our "tribes"—it's easy to get lost in the noise and miss the broader picture. To compensate, our brains lead us to "simplify" the data by choosing a filter and putting our faith in a single position. From there, we create a clean story to match.

Poor Data Analysis

Even if we somehow manage to collect meaningful data without first filtering it through one lens or another, we may still fail to find enduring meaning in all of this information. Proper analysis of the data continues to elude us because our brains struggle *not* to jump to conclusions. For our ancestors, those who were able to apply interpretation fast (e.g., *I should run away from glowing eyes in the night because they are usually dangerous predators*) "won" by surviving and reproducing most successfully.

In an interview with the *Washington Post*, Professor Paul Smith, a social statistician at the University of Southampton, said this about our need to tell stories with data: "We are primates evolved to gather fruit in the forest and when possible to reproduce. So this leaping to conclusions is a good strategy given that the choices are simple and nothing complicated is going on. But at the level of major social policy choices, [jumping to conclusions] is a serious concern."

When it comes to our more complicated modern world, which holds any number of extraneous factors that we can (and should!) measure to paint a more accurate story, a 2018 Forrester Research report summarizes our catastrophic relationship with data perfectly: "We are drowning in data but starving for insights." We may be wired to see patterns, yet very few of us are trained statisticians. The more overwhelmed we become the more we scramble to make sense of it all—often to our detriment.

For example, humans naturally confuse correlation with cause and effect. We pull together spurious correlations in an attempt to make sense of two variables. The more granular the data we have to measure, the more patterns will appear—even if the patterns are no more than flukes.

In a humorous interpretation of this phenomenon, Tyler Vigen, a student at Harvard Law School, used large, public data sets to point out some ridiculous random asso-

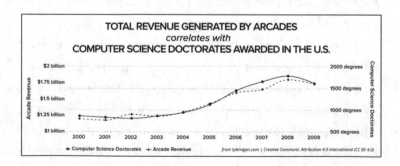

ciations. Who knew, for instance, that the divorce rate in Maine correlates with the per capita consumption of margarine at a rate of 99 percent. It's enough to make any married resident of Maine consider a switch to butter!

In another example, Vigen found a 99 percent correlation between the total revenue generated by arcades and the number of computer science doctorates awarded in the United States. It's tempting to conclude that arcades must influence young players to pursue higher education in a closely related field. But that would be our information-foraging instinct leading us astray.

Even the smartest scientists, doctors, and researchers get caught in spurious correlations. Consider the last time you went to see your physician for a physical. You've probably heard about HDL or "good cholesterol" and LDL or "bad cholesterol." Because HDL is associated with lower rates of heart disease, it seems logical to believe that drugs that raise HDL cholesterol would lead to positive outcomes. But in a clinical trial conducted by the National Heart, Lung, and Blood Institute, which prescribed niacin to raise patients' HDL, researchers had to

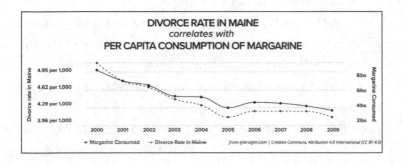

cut the experiment short when it did not reduce the risk of heart attacks in these subjects. It turns out that HDL is simply a *byproduct* of a healthy heart, not a causal factor in heart health.

These are exactly the fallacies we all have to be on the lookout for. Without careful interpretation, we can too easily fall prey to junk data, applying data-driven "solutions" that only serve to reinforce false narratives. After all, no married resident of Maine needs a prescription for butter!

Poor Data Application

When it comes to data application, we need to be in the driver's seat *from the start*. Because if we are unclear about *why and how* we intend to apply the data we are collecting, we risk becoming victims of our own data-collecting instinct, getting hits of dopamine as a reward, but not learning or growing from our efforts. As Lewis Carroll so aptly noted, "If you don't know where you are going, any road will get you there."

One of the most blatant displays of our data instinct gone awry was in the controversy over the use of masks during the COVID-19 pandemic. COVID-19 created a special challenge because it evoked both our instincts of belonging and fear of the other. In a classic display of poor data collection, one "tribe" fed on a source of information that implied that masks were an unnecessary precaution, while ignoring scientific data that showed that wearing masks played an important role in stopping the spread of the virus. This tribe sometimes went so far as to claim that masks were *detrimental* to one's health, making spurious correlations without proper causation data. Meanwhile, another "tribe" insisted that masks needed to be worn at all times to flatten the curve.

Rather than clearly defining the purpose of collecting and interpreting mask-wearing data from the start (i.e., presumably to achieve the best health outcomes for all), we allowed our instincts to drive us to two separate corners of the mat. Where we might have had an opportunity to come together to fight a common external enemy (COVID-19), instead our data-collection instinct (unconcerned with truth but happy to gather information) took the reins.

Working in conjunction with our instinct to belong (and fear the other), we found data to justify our tribe's beliefs while demonizing another tribe's beliefs, never pausing to consider that the two "tribes" could be united around a common purpose. When data are applied poorly, there is no winner. Having a clearly defined question from the start prevents us from meandering down these paths of poor data collection, interpretation, and application.

The question anyone is looking to answer is up to each organization and individual to define. But we have to be clear about the question before we collect our first piece of data. That's where purpose comes into place. Our purpose drives the question, which in turn drives the data. If our purpose, for example, is to serve our customers, the question to ask is: *How can we best serve?* We don't decide in advance that customers will be best served by one thing or another and then focus on the data that support our conclusions. Our ~~purpose~~ purpose cannot be defined by the data, whether we are running multi-billion-dollar companies, a large household, or our own daily lives.

When data are driving, it's easy to take a turn down a path that doesn't align with our values, ignoring good data that didn't support our position, or giving too much sway to those data that do. But by defining purpose at the start, we allow questions to be asked that invite an openness to any and all data that come in. As Ted Sarandos, the chief content officer of Netflix, warns us, "You have to be very cautious not to get caught in the math, because you'll end up making the same thing over and over again." A focus on mission and purpose has kept Netflix from falling prey to a heavy reliance on algorithms and kept them from being creatively stunted. Despite the massive amounts of input that Netflix generates from its 183 million-plus subscribers, its promise, vis-à-vis its own mission statement—to provide "stellar service"—has remained the driving factor that allows Netflix to continually break out from traditional molds with fresh, customer-driven content. Netflix keeps its focus on the mission and the question always at the front of mind: *How are we providing stellar service?* The answers might change based on new data, but the purpose and question does not.

In fact, Netflix recently made a major change to the way it delivered content. Previously, it automatically played trailers on its site, but by 2020 that function became optional. In a tweet, Netflix said, "We've heard the feedback loud and clear—members can now control whether or not they see autoplay previews..." Netflix started collecting, analyzing, and *applying* data in ways that mattered as defined by its purpose: "stellar customer service."

Years ago, I was a faculty member at a boarding school where staff grappled with the data-collection instinct, perhaps with a little less grace than Netflix. I remember spending many hours in meetings where we debated such important topics as whether or not to offer more college courses, changes to grading protocols, how much homework we should assign, and more. Inevitably the conversation would get heated as faculty and administrators threw out numbers and statistics to prove their points. It often required a reminder, and reexamination, of our core purpose in order to resolve these ever-escalating conflicts.

Our decisions were more efficient and solvable when we remembered to ask *first* about purpose: *Do these policies serve our students?* From there, it was a matter of collecting the *right* data to answer the purpose-driven question. Without clarity of purpose, any of our decisions could have been made in any direction. If our purpose was to make the most money, for instance, or recruit the most students or put the most students into the best schools, we could easily have made different choices. But by having a clear vision of our purpose first, we could then decide which individual data was important to collect and analyze for our best results. Without those original principles in place, our ventures would ultimately have failed. Which is precisely the situation in which Tesco had found itself. Management lost hold of their purpose—to serve their customers—and started blindly following the data, even when it strayed from the company's core values.

Death Days and the Joy of Missing Out

We can all do better to keep our data-collection tendencies to a healthy level, both personally and professionally. To do this, we have to start with the end in mind. By beginning with *how* we want to apply the data we're collecting, it will force us to clearly define our goals. Only then can we establish the data we *need* to collect and analyze to serve that purpose.

So let's start with the ultimate end in mind that applies to all of us: You are going to die. How's that for a bitter taste of reality?

Ironically it seems that the only time any of us consistently focuses on purpose is when we are told our time on earth is short. We become instinctually purpose-driven rather than data-driven beings.

So here is my gift to you—a prescription of sorts. You are going to die. I hope not for a very long time, but it is a reality that we all face. Why not start living that reality now and take some *death days*. These are days when you remind yourself that you are in fact mortal and already have, for all intents and purposes, been given the terminal diagnosis that each of us fears.

I first heard of the concept of death days from a TED Talk by Ricardo Semler, the CEO of the highly successful model for industrial democracy, Semco Partners. Semler refers to these days as his "terminal days," during which he does whatever he would be doing if he had a limited amount of time left on earth.

On your death days, spend time with family, travel if you can, and get to the items on your bucket list. More than likely, when the time does come and you get a real diagnosis, you'll be too sick or feeble to tackle your bucket list. So why not schedule them in now? Make time to step back from the day-to-day busy—to zoom out and remember what's truly important. Otherwise, life will plan itself for you while you're busy being busy. Take the time now to help define how you will live a purpose-driven life.

I've found these questions to be particularly helpful to my own defining process:

- What is truly important that I must achieve?
- How do I want myself and/or my organization to be remembered?

- Who do I serve?
- How do I make the world a better place?
- What will I do to make myself, my children or parents, my customers, and my eight-year-old-self proud?

Purpose is where you need to spend 90 percent of your focus and drive. Your purpose points to the data you need to collect and analyze in order to achieve your own definition of greatness.

It will be tempting to chase other opportunities and leads. Every shiny object might be rewarding in its own right. But ask yourself first if it is data that will help you further your goals. If not, then prioritize your time and focus or you'll quickly find yourself running in circles of data that may or may not be pertinent to your larger aspirations.

After narrowing focus to the data that will support and serve only your purpose, you're likely to experience anxiety over the fear of missing out (also known as FOMO). When I first launched my business, I found my own FOMO to be particularly challenging. Every phone call, every person who wanted to meet for free consulting or to do another activity that wasn't strictly focused on my mission—these *felt* like they could be good opportunities. I was so terrified of missing out on important data (in the form of a connection or lead that would really push my purpose forward), that I ended up giving in to my data-collecting instinct. I spent my days fulfilling other people's needs, without getting any of the deep work done that I needed to do in order to advance my own goals. I was allowing the wrong data to drive. Instead of chasing quality data, I was collecting clutter.

When I finally made my purpose clear, I was able to say "no" more readily to opportunities that did not directly advance it. I even reframed FOMO into JOMO (joy of missing out). Knowing that I missed out on a distraction helped me be more productive and joyful at the task I had chosen to undertake instead.

One way to better experience JOMO is to schedule *literally* every minute of your day into a calendar. Schedule time for meetings, calls, answering emails, having a snack, television, working out, social media scrolling, sleeping, playing with your dog—whatever it is you plan to do over the next twenty-four hours. Repeat this for seven days. What you'll quickly realize as you move through your week is that time spent doing things outside of your schedule impedes on time for another opportunity that *is* scheduled. Each time your data-hungry instinct pulls you to seek more data from one part of your day, you'll be forced to confront that this urge will squelch out time you had allotted for another activity. Doing a full-out audit of your time helps you to focus on the information you *need* to be collecting, rather than getting trapped in emails or social posts for hours, stuck in an information-gathering dopamine-loop.

It's not up to me to define purpose or joy for you. It's completely fine if your joy is spending five hours a day scrolling through social media. Just be sure to schedule that time into your day (rather than a walk, or time with family, or anything that typically brings *me* joy). And schedule your time with intention so that you are truly collecting data that serve you, rather than bowing to your instincts that cause you to serve the data.

With purpose and data input refined, our focus finally shifts to interpretation. It's easy to fall into old patterns of "filling in the blanks" when even a hint of a relationship or pattern exists in data. A classic study conducted on college students demonstrated just how eager we are to interpret data as meaningful. Fritz Heider and Marianne Simmel at Smith College showed thirty-four students a movie clip in which three shapes (two triangles and a circle) moved around while a rectangle remained motionless on the screen. The students were then asked to describe what they saw. All but one student applied emotion and meaning to what they had seen. Rather than random shapes floating about the screen, they suggested that the shapes were "worried" or "innocent" or "blinded by rage."

Creating patterns from chaos is how we give ourselves a sense of control over the world—it's how we give our lives meaning. But what would happen if we stopped trying to control the narrative—stopped trying to bend it toward us "winning" the debate? What if instead we were more curious about another's perspective rather than leaping to conclusions or judgment? Perhaps if we were willing to engage in a steel-person approach (testing and collecting data on the best arguments of an alternative perspective), rather than associating another's interpretation with malevolence, we might learn to see and appreciate more of life.

By controlling our instinct to collect data, our organizations and our personal lives will flourish. Remember that no amount of information will ever satisfy our thirsty brains. But just as we've discovered with all the other instincts explored in this book, every one of us has the power to take back control of our biological drives. There is no FOMO when it comes to death. This very knowledge can help us to guide our instincts toward collecting our most joyful, useful data in life.

Chapter 7: Key Takeaways

- Be willing to consider information that doesn't support your perspective.
- Double-check that you aren't falling into the fallacy of correlation implying causation.
- Keep it simple—"real leaders don't need clutter."
- Identify your purpose-driven question first and allow it to inform decisions on how data should be applied.
- Eliminate FOMO by reframing into JOMO.
- Schedule Death Days.
- Be curious and set up steel-person arguments rather than associating negative stories to data interpreted differently than your story.

Becoming Fear(less)

A student once asked his Zen master, "Why would the Japanese make such delicate and thin teacups? They break far too easily." The master replied, "It's not that they're too delicate, but that you don't know how to handle them. You must adjust yourself to the environment, and not vice versa." (From *To Shine One Corner of the World: Moments with Shunryu Suzuki—Stories of a Zen Teacher Told by His Students*, edited by David Chadwick.)

IN MANY WAYS, HUMANS HAVE reshaped our environments to better suit our needs (air-conditioning, cars, grocery stores). Yet our brains are indeed delicate teacups in the crushing maw of the modern world in which we live. We don't want to cease the technological and cultural progress that has shaped our society to be so advanced, but we must find ways to more delicately handle the teacup brains we have brought along for the ride. Without a focused and conscious intervention, instincts that once resolved our greatest issues will, in our modern lives, continue to disrupt our productivity and happiness. But it doesn't have to be that way. We all have the power to intervene and rewire our instincts.

My father was a minister for most of his life. While I remember very little about my time spent in the hard church pews, I do remember one particular Sunday sermon. Dad stood in front of his congregation with a bottle full of water. He uncapped it and began shaking the bottle violently, water splashing everywhere. My eyes widened. I remember thinking that things at church had suddenly gotten very interesting.

My father then asked his congregation what I thought was a deceptively simple question: "Why does the water spill out?" As he stood there at the front, still shaking the nearly empty bottle, he answered that water spilled out because it was water that was inside. "What spills out of you?" he continued. "When life shakes you, which it inevitably will, what will spill out?"

I believe that the answer for most of us is *instincts*. Instincts spill out in the form of fear, biases, deceptions, stories, and behaviors we wouldn't consciously want to be exhibiting and acting on. If we don't take the time (which each of us *does* have), to begin intervening in our own instincts, we aren't being the fully conscious, capable humans that we are meant to be.

Our brains were designed to keep us safe, and they have done just that for hundreds of thousands of years. But today they are preventing us from fully living. Without intervening we aren't making conscious choices. We are just obeying and following the shortcuts that have already been written for us. We are more than our instincts. We deserve to write a better story and it begins with the interventions in this book—interventions that will help all of us to become fear(less).

You'll note that "less" is in parentheses. That's because I don't necessarily think being *fearless* is a good strategy. Walking out in front of a bus because you don't fear it is a bad choice any way you cut it. But actively and consciously deciding what deserves your fear—that's real power. That's you moving beyond your subconscious instincts to a *super*conscious state of being.

Moving beyond subconscious instincts is going to be even more important as we face a changing world. As of this writing, in the fall of 2020, the COVID-19 pandemic has forced many businesses and institutions to close, individuals to isolate, and those fortunate to have employment to find creative ways to work from home while juggling personal responsibilities. Our primitive survival directives are in full force, as we try to protect our "tribes," by raiding supermarkets, stockpiling toilet paper, and leaving the news on twenty-four hours a day to collect more information that ultimately isn't likely to be useful. Now, more than ever, we need to use our conscious brains to keep our families and organizations safe and thriving.

We are all making decisions that have the potential to impact the lives of everyone on our teams, in our families, and across our communities. This responsibility can be a daunting weight to carry even in the best of times. But when we have drastic disruptions to our lives, such as those imposed by COVID-19, the burden can become crushing. Now more than ever we need to find ways to pause, think, and then act effectively, responsibly, and empathetically, while avoiding the behavioral pitfalls to which our instincts will direct us. We need to be real about risks without leaping immediately to a panicked, instinctual, full-of-fear response.

Here are the three most common instinct-driven behavioral pitfalls I've seen people flounder with during this unprecedented crisis, as well as ways for you to avoid their mistakes:

Fear(full) Response 1: The Short-Term Solver

Under times of extended stress, we naturally limit the options we will consider. Instead of opening our eyes to all possibilities, it's human nature to put on blinders and return to the rules we know—or at least the rules we *think* we know.

Our brains actually undergo scientifically demonstrated *cognitive impairment* (e.g., impaired memory, impaired creativity, impaired decision-making) in times when we need them the most. This is nature's way of "saving us," by reducing the tremendous amount of energy our brains would be consuming by thinking. Instead, our biology redirects us to rely solely on instinct. And as you now know, the message our instincts send us is clear: "*Survive. Nothing else matters but NOW.*"

Instead of quickly solving a problem for the short term, a more fear(less) response would be to *flip the narrative and look to the long term*. Ask: "What does this problem look like in twelve months?" Fixing an immediate issue in an uncertain environment might mean that tomorrow there is an entirely new issue, or that the issue you "fixed" wasn't actually an issue at all. By flipping the narrative and keeping a long-term perspective, you can ensure you are more prepared as situations evolve, rather than accepting what feels like a static short-term solution.

Fear(full) Response 2: The Ego-Enhancer

Another instinctual response to uncertainty is to reestablish ourselves as experts and authority figures. No doubt we all appreciate clear information and guidance. But when we are facing unprecedented situations in which some basic questions (*How long will this last?*) are unanswerable, it is far more damaging to pretend we have the answers when the reality is that we simply aren't equipped or informed any more than most. It's essential for us to show up to our families and teams with intention, but also with vulnerability. It's okay to not have all the answers. In fact, being willing to admit that is often exactly what people need to hear. It exhibits empathy, while allowing you to exemplify the calm emotional stability that's needed during turbulent times.

We can lead powerfully while expressing our doubt or uncertainty—the greatest leaders do. In fact, times of crisis require *humility*. Rather than losing trust by passing along information that may be inaccurate, approach issues from the vulnerable position of the non-expert. This shows that you are more likely to seek out credible sources of information. Confident leadership requires sorting what we do and do not know and distilling that message to clear, accurate communications.

As I mentioned in an earlier chapter, my friend and mentor Artie Isaac keeps a Post-it note tacked to his computer screen where he is sure to see it every day. The note reads: "This is your captain speaking." It reminds Artie of the clear, calm voice with which he wants to speak to his friends, colleagues, and family.

You've likely had the unpleasant experience of a turbulent plane ride, but for those who may have missed it, imagine a roller coaster in the air that you truly don't want to be on. During bumpy rides, it's highly unlikely that your captain's voice comes on to the loudspeaker shouting, "Ahhhhhhh, I don't know what's happening! Things are scary!" That would be truly terrifying. She also probably doesn't come on saying, "I know exactly what's happening here. I'm doing this on purpose. Enjoy the ride!" Arguably that announcement might be even scarier.

Instead, she calmly announces, "This is your captain speaking," and proceeds to state in a clear and calm voice: (1) what she knows ("We are experiencing a bit of turbulence at the moment"); (2) what she doesn't know ("It isn't exactly clear when we will be out of this bumpy air"); and (3) the actions she is taking to get answers and resolve the issue ("We've contacted air traffic control to try and find us some smoother air soon, and we will let you know when we have further information").

We all want to be experts. We all want to remove pains from our teams and especially from those we love. But sometimes, the kindest thing we can do is to be clear. The more comfortable we are with communicating what we don't know, the more trust we will build and the easier everyone around us can endure the turbulent times.

Fear(full) Response 3: The Hideaway

Uncertainty can paralyze us. In stressful times, when we feel like our thinking is unclear, our instincts signal for us to retreat or freeze. Rather than face others while feeling scattered, we reduce or halt communication completely until we have a better grasp of the situation. Think about how detrimental this could be for people who are looking to you for answers.

Ambiguous situations require the exact opposite of this fear(full) response. As leaders to our employees and our families, we need to communicate and be present even more than normal. To them, the only thing more frustrating than not knowing what's happening is feeling like you are avoiding them. While the information we convey might not help resolve issues, being communicated to alleviates their feelings of being forgotten or abandoned in a tenuous situation.

Imagine if on the turbulent plane you simply never heard from your captain! You might think the trouble was far worse and you'd spiral deeper into unproductive behaviors. Ignoring issues only makes them grow larger in the eyes of those around us. The communication the pilot gives might not get us where we need to go any faster or smoother, but it makes us feel a bit better knowing we are in it together. Our communities don't need us to have all the answers, or solutions right away, but they need us to communicate frequently to help quell their own fears.

Placing blame or pointing fingers at others for failing to respond effectively is also unproductive. Sure, we all engage in at least some of these fear(full) responses any time there is a major upheaval in our environment. But we have the option to consciously do better—to resist our biological defaults. Fear(full) times call for fear(less) leadership. You have the power to override your instincts and be the leader your team and family need, no matter what turbulent times we experience.

One of my favorite quotes, attributed to Charles Darwin, recognizes that "It's not the strongest nor the smartest of the species that survive, but those that are most adaptable." This quote is brimming with hope. The hope that we, too, have the ability—if not the responsibility—to change and grow.

Something rare happened in our evolutionary history: We humans managed to remove ourselves from the day-to-day pressures of natural selection. We no longer daily need to fight for our very survival. As such, human beings have achieved an unprecedented level of freedom—this is utterly unique in the animal world.

The fact that we can reshape and rewire our own brains across time and remove ourselves from natural selection means that we already possess an incredible amount of power and control in our hands. What we choose to do with that power is entirely up to us. What will you do when you take back control from your instincts?

Sources

Introduction

p. xii **Claremont Graduate University's Distinguished Professor**

Why It's So Hard to Pay Attention, Explained by Science. Retrieved 11/13/20 from www.fastcompany.com.

CHAPTER 1—SURVIVAL: MAKING HASTE, SLOWLY

p. 3 **But in other scenarios**

Keegan, S. "Lost hiker eats beloved pet dog who saved his life in desperate bid to survive in Canadian wilderness." *Daily Mirror* (U.K.), November 2, 2013.

p. 3 **A strong survival instinct**

C. Colson, D. Boyle, J. Smithson, S. Beaufoy, et al., *127 Hours*. Twentieth Century Fox Home Entertainment, 2010.

p. 5 **One day in January 2017**

Gene Weingarten, "Pearls Before Breakfast: Can One of the Nation's Great Musicians Cut through the Fog of a D.C. Rush Hour? Let's Find Out." *Washington Post*, April 8, 2007.

p. 9   **Stress has been called**
Eric Fink, "Stress: The Health Epidemic of the 21st Century." scitechconnect.elsevier.com/stress-health-epidemic-21st-century.

p. 11   **Corporate America endures**
Abend, L. (2019). Financial stress and its cost. Retrieved 11/13/20 from retirement.johnhancock.com/us/en/viewpoints/financial-wellness/financial-stress-what-s-the-cost.

p. 11   **So it's no surprise**
Kathyrn Mayer, "HRE's Number of the Day: Coronavirus Stress." hrexecutive.com/hres-number-of-the-day-coronavirus-stress.

p. 11   **Approximately 88 percent of workers**
Mayer, K. Employee stress levels caused by COVID19. Retrieved 11/13/20 from hrexecutive.com/hres-number-of-the-day-coronavirus-stress.

p. 12   **A 2018 study published in *Neurology***
Justin B. Echouffo-Tcheugui, Sarah C. Conner, Jayandra J. Himali, et al. Circulating cortisol and cognitive and structural brain measures: The Framingham Heart Study. *Neurology, 91,* 21 (Nov. 2018).

p. 12   **Separate peer-reviewed scientific studies**
F. C. Hsu, M. J. Garside, A. E. Massey, and R. H. McAllister-Williams, Effects of a Single Dose of Cortisol on the Neural Correlates of Episodic Memory and Error Processing in Healthy Volunteers, *Psychopharmacology* 167 (2003): 431–42; Cueva, C., Roberts, R., Spencer, T. et al. Cortisol and testosterone increase financial risk taking and may destabilize markets. *Scientific Reports (Nature), 5,* 11206 (2015).

p. 12   Participants in a 2016 study

Starcke K, Wiesen C, Trotzke P, Brand M. Effects of Acute Laboratory Stress on Executive Functions. *Frontiers in Psychology* 7, 461.

p. 19   When Einstein first published

"Scientist Explained His Theory With Wit and Homey Parables." *New York Times*, April 19, 1955, p. 26, col. 3.

p. 20   Psychologist Aoife McLoughlin

Fiona MacDonald, "Science Says That Technology Is Speeding Up Our Brains' Perception of Time." *Science Alert*, November 19, 2015.

p. 20   Additional research finds

Perception of Time Pressure Impairs Performance. ScienceDaily, February 16, 2009.

p. 21   Georgetown University professor

Cal Newport, *Deep Work: Rules for Focused Success in a Distracted World.* New York: Grand Central, 2016.

p. 21   Gloria Mark's empirical study

Mark, G. et al. "The cost of interrupted work: more speed and stress." *Computer Human Interaction* (2008).

p. 22   A University of California–Irvine study

González, V. M., and Mark, G. "Constant, Constant, Multi-tasking Craziness": Managing Multiple Working Spheres. *Proceedings of the SIGCHI Conference on Human Factors in Computing Systems* (April 2004), 133–20.

p. 22   Another study found that 70 percent

Jackson, T., Dawson, R., and Wilson, D. The Cost of Email Interruption. *Journal of Systems and Information Technology, 5,* 1 (2004).

p. 22   **And, according to a study from Carnegie Mellon**
Bob Sullivan and Hugh Thompson. *The Plateau Effect: Getting from Stuck to Success.* New York: Dutton, 2013. [Excerpted with permission from the publisher. All Rights Reserved.]

p. 23   **"The brain goes through a lot of trouble"**
Healy, M.. Memory, emotions can trip up time perceptions. *Los Angeles Times*, March 9, 2009.

p. 25   **"For 42 years"**
Couric, K. Capt. "Sully Worried About Airline Industry." CBS News, February 10, 2009.

p. 30   **"Most people have the capacity"**
Bell, J. "'Anxious' or 'excited'? How to find your stress sweet spot." *Irish Times,* August 29, 2017.

CHAPTER 2—SEX: REDEFINING ROLES, LEADERSHIP, AND RESPONSIBILITY

p. 39   **Amazingly, in studies**
Nave, G., Nadler, A., Dubois, D., et al. Single-dose testosterone administration increases men's preference for status goods. *Nature Communnications, 9,* 2433 (2018).

p. 40   **A 2013 study found that men**
Stulp, G., Buunk, A. P., Verhulst, S., and Pollet, T. V. Tall claims? Sense and nonsense about the importance of height of US presidents. *Leadership Quarterly* (2013).

p. 40   **The aggregated data**
Ibid.

p. 43   **A study published in *Personnel Psychology***
Ena Inesi and Daniel Cable. "When Accomplishments Come Back to Haunt You: The Negative Effect of

Competence Signals on Women's Performance Evaluations." *Personnel Psychology* (2014).

p. 43 Another team of researchers

Leah D. Sheppard et al., "A Man's (Precarious) Place: Men's Experienced Threat and Self-Assertive Reactions to Female Superiors," *Personality and Social Psychology Bulletin* (July 2015).

p. 44 Despite evidence from a 2011 Zenger Folkman survey

Zenger, J., and Folkman, J.). "Research: Women Score Higher Than Men in Most Leadership Skills." *Harvard Business Review*, June 25, 2019.

p. 45 A Harvard and U.S. Naval Academy study

Phillips, B. L., Mehay, S. L., and Bowman, W. R. *An Analysis of the Effect of Quantitative and Qualitative Admissions Factors in Determining Student Performance at the U.S. Naval Academy*. (2004). Retrieved from apps.dtic.mil/sti/citations/ADA427695.

p. 45 But as a 2019 article in *Bloomberg Businessweek*

Greenfield, R. "Having More Women CEOs Won't Fix the Gender Gap." *Bloomberg Businessweek*, December 12, 2019.

p. 48 In June 2018, Ernst & Young

Folley, A. (2019). Ernst & Young catches heat over reported training exercise advising women on how to dress, act around men. TheHill, October 21, 2019.

p. 48 In 2017, a year before

Wakabayashi, D. "Contentious Memo Strikes Nerve Inside Google and Out." *New York Times*, August 8, 2017.

p. 50   One striking example

Beilock, S. L., Rydell, R. J., and McConnell, A. R. Stereotype Threat and Working Memory: Mechanisms, Alleviation, and Spillover. *Journal of Experimental Psychology: General, 136,* 2, (2007), 256–76.

p. 58   In fact, between 2015 and 2019

Data Visualizations: Sexual Harassment Charge Data U.S. Equal Employment Opportunity Commission. (n.d.).

p. 59   A 2003 study published

M. G. Haselton, "The Sexual Overperception Bias: Evidence of a Systematic Bias in Men from a Survey of Naturally Occurring Events, *Journal of Research in Personality, 37* (2003), 34–47.

p. 60   A 2018 study on "Predicting"

Woerner, Jacqueline et al. "Predicting Men's Immediate Reactions to a Simulated Date's Sexual Rejection: The Effects of Hostile Masculinity, Impersonal Sex, and Hostile Perceptions of the Woman." *Psychology of Violence, 8,* 3 (2018), 349–57.

p. 61   In a revealing 2001 study

Woodzicka, J. A., and LaFrance, M. (2001), Real Versus Imagined Gender Harassment. *Journal of Social Issues, 57,* 15–30.

p. 62   Researcher George Loewenstein

Loewenstein, G. Hot-Cold Empathy Gaps and Medical Decision Making. *Health Psychology, 24,* 4 (Suppl.) (2005), 549–56.

p. 69   In 2019, a study out of Cornell

Duffy, B. E., and Hund, E. Gendered Visibility on Social Media: Navigating Instagram's Authenticity Bind. *International Journal of Communication, 13* (2019).

p. 69   A 2013 study found

Pierce, L., Dahl, M. S., and Nielsen, J. In Sickness and in Wealth: Psychological and Sexual Costs of Income Comparison in Marriage. *Personality and Social Psychology Bulletin*, *39*, 3, (2013), 359–74.

p. 71   Psychology professor Julie Woodzicka

Lafrance, Marianne, and Woodzicka, Julie. "Prejudice: The Target's Perspective." In *No laughing matter: Women's verbal and nonverbal reactions to sexist humor.* (1998).

p. 72   One recent study found

Bradley Ruffle and Ze'ev Shtudiner. "Are Good-Looking People More Employable?" No. 1006, Working Papers,Ben-Gurion University of the Negev, Department of Economics, 2010.

p. 73   In a study that's achieved

Goldin, Claudia, and Cecilia Rouse. "Orchestrating Impartiality: The Impact of 'Blind' Auditions on Female Musicians." *American Economic Review*, *90*, 4, (2000), 715–41.

p. 74   That may seem a little silly

Klofstad, C.A., Anderson, R. C., and Peters, S. Sounds like a winner: voice pitch influences perception of leadership capacity in both men and women. *Proceedings of the. Royal Society Bulletin*, *279* (2012), 2698–2704.

p. 75   Corinne Moss-Racusin, a psychology

Moss-Racusin, C.A., and Rudman, L.A. Disruptions in Women's Self-Promotion: The Backlash Avoidance Model. *Psychology of Women Quarterly*, *34* (2010), 186–202; Laurie A. Rudman, Corinne A. Moss-

Racusin, Julie E. Phelan, Sanne Nauts. Status incongruity and backlash effects: Defending the gender hierarchy motivates prejudice against female leaders. *Journal of Experimental Social Psychology, 48*, 1 (2012), 165–79.

p. 75   Additional research has found

Judge, T. A., Livingston, B. A., and Hurst, C. Do nice guys—and gals—really finish last? The joint effects of sex and agreeableness on income. *Journal of Personality and Social Psychology, 102*, 2 (2012), 390–407.

CHAPTER 3—VARIETY: THE SURPRISING SATISFACTION OF LESS

p. 79   But between the years 2008 and 2010

Davis, J. "How Lego clicked: the brand that reinvented itself." *Guardian*, June 4, 2017.

p. 83   Researchers Margo Wilson and Martin Daly

Martin Daly and Margo Wilson. Crime and Conflict: Homicide in Evolutionary Psychological Perspective. *Crime and Justice, 22* (1997), 51–100

p. 83   The "marshmallow tests"

Walter Mischel and Ebbe B. Ebbesen. "Attention in Delay of Gratification." *Journal of Personality and Social Psychology, 16*, 2 (1970), 329–37.

p. 84   A 2011 follow-up

B. J. Casey, Leah H. Somerville, Ian H. Gotlib, Ozlem Ayduk, et al. "From the Cover: Behavioral and Neural Correlates of Delay of Gratification 40 Years Later." *Proceedings of the National Academy of Sciences, 108*, 36 (August 29, 2011), 14998–15003.

p. 88   **A study from Cornell University**
Wansink, B., and Sobal, J. Mindless Eating: The 200 Daily Food Decisions We Overlook. *Environment and Behavior, 39*, 1 (2007), 106–23.

p. 89   **MIT neuroscientist Earl K. Miller**
Korkki, P. "Business Guides: How to Improve Your Productivity at Work." *New York Times*.

p. 91   **In one study from Columbia and Stanford**
Iyengar, S. S., and Lepper, M. R. (2000). When Choice Is Demotivating: Can One Desire Too Much of a Good Thing? doi.org/10.1037/0022-3514.79.6.995.

p. 92   **According to a Gallup report**
Kelly, J. "More Than Half of U.S. Workers Are Unhappy in Their Jobs: Here's Why and What Needs to Be Done Now." *Forbes,* October 25, 2019; Not Just a Job: Quality of Work in the U.S. (2019). Retrieved 11/13/20, from www.gallup.com/education/267590/great-jobs-lumina-gates-omidyar-gallup-report-2019.aspx.

p. 92   **Our slide into dissatisfaction**
Kan, M., Levanon, G., Li, A., and Ray, R. L. (2017). Job Satisfaction: More Opportunity and Job Satisfaction in a Tighter Labor Market. Retrieved from www.conferenceboard.org.

p. 92   **While science has repeatedly shown**
Doheny, K. Clutter Control: Is Too Much "Stuff" Draining You? Retrieved 11/13/20 from www.webmd.com/balance/features/clutter-control#1; Rong Wang, Hongyun Liu, Jiang Jiang, and Yue Song. Will materialism lead to happiness? A longitudinal analysis of the mediating role of psychological needs satisfaction. *Personality and Individual Differences, 105* (2017), 312–17;

Froh, J. J., Emmons, R. A., Card, N. A., et al. Gratitude
and the Reduced Costs of Materialism in Adolescents.
*Journal of Happiness Stud*ies, *12*, (2011), 289–302.

p. 94   Our biology confirms the rewards

Joseph, P. N., Sharma, R. K., Agarwal, A., et al. Men
Ejaculate Larger Volumes of Semen, More Motile
Sperm, and More Quickly When Exposed to Images of
Novel Women. *Evolutionary Psychological Science, 1*
(2015), 195–200.

p. 95   The late behavioral economist Herbert Simon

Simon, H. *Administrative Behavior: A Study of Decision-Making Processes in Administrative Organization.*
New York: Macmillan, 1947.

p. 99   Their results demonstrated

Schwartz, B., Ward, A., Monterosso, J., et al. Maximizing versus satisficing: Happiness is a matter of
choice. *Journal of Personality and Social Psychology, 83*, 5
(Nov. 2002), 1178–97.

p. 99   Another study published

Iyengar, S. S., Wells, R. E., and Schwartz, B. "Doing
Better but Feeling Worse: Looking for the 'Best' Job Undermines Satisfaction." *Psychological Science, 17*, 3 (2006),
143–50.

p. 101   Studies have found that when we buy

Dvorsky, G.. The 12 cognitive biases that prevent you
from being rational (2013). Retrieved from io9.com/
5974468/the-most-common-cognitive-biases-that-pre-
vent-you-from-being-rational.

p. 102   Rabbi Hyman Schachtel declared

H. J. Schachtel, *The Real Enjoyment of Living*. New
York: Dutton, 1954, 37.

p. 104 Five Guys ranked first

Britain's Favourite Fast-Food Restaurants and Coffee Shops Revealed. Market Force Information (marketforce.com), March 21, 2016.

CHAPTER 4—SELF-DECEPTION: I KNOW YOU ARE, BUT WHAT AM I?

p. 108 Words, objects, or pictures

Wolman, D. "A tale of two halves." *Nature*, March 15, 2012.

p. 109 Neuroscientist Benjamin Libet

Libet, B. Unconscious cerebral initiative and the role of conscious will in voluntary action. *Behavioral and Brain Sciences*, *8*, 4 (1985), 529–39.

p. 110 Twenty years later, using fMRI

Chun Siong Soon, Marcel Brass, Hans-Jochen Heinze, and John-Dylan Haynes. "Unconscious Determinants of Free Decisions in the Human Brain" *Nature Neuroscience*, April 13, 2008.

p. 112 As economist Robin Hanson explains

Simler, K., and Hanson, R. *The Elephant in the Brain: Hidden Motives in Everyday Life*. Oxford University Press, 2018; 80,000 Hours Podcast: Why we have to lie to ourselves about why we do what we do (2020).

p. 114 "Research has linked telling lies"

Meyers, L. "White lies intended to be innocent still have potential to harm." *Kansas State Collegian*, April 25, 2014.

p. 114 As science historian Oren Harman explains

Harman, O. "Does Biology Make Us Liars?" *New Republic*, October 5, 2012.

p. 115 Turns out there is scientific evidence

H. E. Adams, L. W. Wright, Jr., and B. A. Lohr, "Is Homophobia Associated with Homosexual Arousal?" *Journal of Abnormal Psychology 105*, 3 (1996), 440–45.

p. 115 Elizabeth Holmes was a Silicon Valley darling

Belluz, J. (2018, March 14). SEC charges Theranos CEO Elizabeth Holmes with fraud. Retrieved 11/13/20 from www.vox.com; Hartmans, A., and Leskin, P. *Business Insider*, August 11, 2020.

p. 116 Dr. Dan Ariely

Ginsberg, L., and Haddleston Jr., T. (2019, March 20). HBO's "The Inventor": How Elizabeth Holmes fooled people about Theranos. Retrieved 11/13/20 from www.cnbc.com.

p. 116 The placebo effect

J. C. Tilburt, E. J. Emanuel, T. J. Kaptchuk, F. A. Curlin, and F. G. Miller. "Prescribing 'Placebo Treatments': Results of National Survey of US Internists and Rheumatologists," *BMJ* [British Medical Journal], *337* (2008), a1938.

p. 117 A 2013 follow-up study

J. Howick, F. L. Bishop, C. Heneghan, J. Wolstenholme, et al. "Placebo Use in the United Kingdom: Results from a National Survey of Primary Care Practitioners," *PLoS* [Public Library of Science] *One*, *8* (2013), e58247.

p. 118   Harvard philosopher

William James. "The Will to Believe." In Steven M. Cahn (ed.), *"The Will to Believe" and Other Essays in Popular Philosophy* (1st pub. New York: Longmans, Green, 1896), 1–15.

p. 118   Dr. Nick Morgan

Morgan, N. Body Language—9. Retrieved 11/13/20 from publicwords.com/2008/05/08/body-language-3.

p. 120   A beloved NBC news reporter

Engel, P., and Bertrand, N. "What Brian Williams has lied about." *Business Insider,* February 13, 2015.

p. 124   In a meta-analysis of sex differences

Balliet, D., Norman Li, A. P., Macfarlan, S. J., and Van Vugt, M. "Sex Differences in Cooperation: A Meta-Analytic Review of Social Dilemmas." *Psychological Bulletin, 137*, 6, (2011), 881–909.

p. 125   The *Challenger* explosion

Berkes, H. "30 Years After Explosion, Challenger Engineer Still Blames Himself." NPR: *All Things Considered*, January 28, 2016; Raval, S. "Challenger: A Management Failure." *Space Safety Magazine*, September 8, 2014; Teitel, A. S. (December 13, 2019). "Challenger Explosion: How Groupthink and Other Causes Led to the Tragedy." Retrieved 11/14/20 from www.history.com.

p. 128   The story of Cliff Young

"Cliff Young—the farmer who outran the field." *Farm Progress* (n.d.).

p. 129   A much cited 2011 article

Pammolli, F., Magazzini, L., and Riccaboni, M. The productivity crisis in pharmaceutical R and D. *Nature Reviews Drug Discovery, 10* (2011), 428–38.

p. 131   A recent scientific paper out of MIT

Lakhani, Karim. "Broadcast Search in Problem Solving: Attracting Solutions from the Periphery, 1." Portland International Conference on Management of Engineering and Technology, 6 (2006), 2450–68.

p. 132   As Bough told *Fast Company*

Sacks, D. "The Story of Oreo: How an Old Cookie Became a Modern Marketing Persona" (October 23, 2014). Retrieved 11/14/20 from www.fastcompany.com.

p. 133   Oreo leveraged social platforms

Ibid.; "Oreo's 'Daily Twist' wins Cannes Cyber Lions Grand Prix." Cannes Lions social media case study (June 21, 2013). Retrieved 11/14/20 from www.digital strategyconsulting.com.

p. 133   Despite the fact that 95 percent

Eurich, T. "What Self-Awareness Really Is (and How to Cultivate It)." *Harvard Business Review*, January 4, 2018; Silvia, P. J., and O'Brien, M. E. Self-awareness and constructive functioning: Revisiting "the human dilemma." *Journal of Social and Clinical Psychology*, (August 2004); Bass, B. M., and Yammarino, F. J. Congruence of Self and Others' Leadership Ratings of Naval Officers for Understanding Successful Performance. *Applied Psychology, 40,* 4, (1991), 437–54; Fletcher, C., and Bailey, C. Assessing self-awareness: Some issues and methods. *Journal of Managerial Psychology, 18,* 5 (2003), 395–404; Sutton, A., Williams, H. M., and Allinson, C. W. A longitudinal, mixed method evaluation of self-awareness training in the workplace. *European Journal of Training and Development, 39,* 7 (2015), 610–27.

p. 133   Roger L. Martin
Martin, R. L. "Management by Imagination." *Harvard Business Review,* January 19, 2010.

p. 135   Naveen Jain
XPRIZE. (n.d.). Retrieved 11/14/20 from www.xprize.org/about/people/naveen-and-anu-jain.

Chapter 6—Belonging: Birds of a Feather Crush Competition Together

p. 143   A 2019 report by BetterUp Labs
BetterUp's New, Industry-Leading Research Shows Companies That Fail at Belonging Lose Tens of Millions in Revenue (September 16, 2019). Retrieved 11/14/20 from www.betterup.com.

p. 145   The natural ability of our brains
H. Taijfel. "Experiments in Intergroup Discrimination," *Scientific American, 223,* 5 (Nov. 1970), 96–102.

p. 154   At its peak in December 2000
Microsoft throws stack ranking out the window (n.d.). Retrieved 11/14/20 from www.impraise.com.

p. 155   A fascinating experiment in the egg
W. M. Muir, "Genetics and the Behaviour of Chickens: Welfare and Productivity." In *Genetics and the Behaviour of Domestic Animals,* 2nd ed. Purdue, 2013, 1–30.

p. 156   While Microsoft was busy dividing
"Apple employees break their vow of secrecy to describe the best—and worst—things about working for Apple." *Business Insider,* December 14, 2016.

p. 157   Debi Coleman
Isaacson, W. "The Real Leadership Lessons of Steve Jobs." *Harvard Business Review,* April 2012.

p. 164   Clever experiments in the lab
David DeSteno, Monica Bartlett, Jolie Wormwood, Lisa Williams, and Leah Dickens, "Gratitude as Moral Sentiment: Emotion-Guided Cooperation in Economic Exchange," *Emotion, 10* (2010), 289–93.

p. 165   Research finds that the act of giving
Aknin, L. B., Dunn, E. W., and Norton, M. I.) Happiness Runs in a Circular Motion: Evidence for a Positive Feedback Loop between Prosocial Spending and Happiness. *Journal of Happiness Studies, 13* (2012), 347–55.

p. 166   Social media tycoon
Vaynerchuk, G. Giving Without Expectation (2015). Retrieved 11/14/20 from www.garyvaynerchuk.com.

p. 167   Harvard researchers have been tracking
Mineo, L. "Over nearly 80 years, Harvard study has been showing how to live a healthy and happy life." *Harvard Gazette*, April 11, 2017.

p. 168   In fact, at least one study
Dunn, E. W., Aknin, L. B., and Norton, M. I. "Spending Money on Others Promotes Happiness." *Science, 319,* 5870 (March 21, 2008), 1687–88.

p. 171   Amid the major revenue declines
Byers, D. "BuzzFeed to cut salaries, CEO to go unpaid." NBC News (n.d.).

p. 171   Chuck Robbins, CEO
King, I. "Cisco CEO Tells Staff Jobs Are Safe, Urges Others to Avoid Cuts." Bloomberg, April 8, 2020.

p. 172   In 1980, Robert Axelrod
Tobin, J. "The prisoner's dilemma." *Michigan Today,*
September 26, 2019.

p. 174   But as research professor and best-selling author
Brown, B. *Rising Strong.* Penguin Random House
Canada, 2015.

CHAPTER 6—FEAR OF THE OTHER: WHY STRANGERS STILL SIGNAL DANGER

p. 180   Reports from McKinsey and Company
Hunt, V., Yee, L., Prince, S., and Dixon-Fyle, S. (2018).
Delivering through diversity. Retrieved www.mckinsey.
com/business-functions/organization/our-insights/
delivering-through-diversity; Hewlett, S. A., Marshall,
M., and Sherbin, L. "How Diversity Can Drive Innova-
tion." *Harvard Business Review,* December 2013; Larson,
E. (2017, September 25). Research Shows Diversity + Inclusion = Better Decision Making at Work. Retrieved
11/14/20 from www.cloverpop.com.

p. 181   A 2020 report from Citigroup
Akala, A. "U.S. Economy Lost $16 Trillion Because of
Racism, Citigroup Says." NPR, October 23, 2020.

p. 181   According to a Deloitte 2018 census
*Missing Pieces Report: The 2018 Board Diversity Cen-
sus of Women and Minorities on Fortune 500 Boards.*
Alliance for Board Diversity, 2018. Retrieved from
www.theabd.org.

p. 181   The *New York Times* reported
Miller, C. C., Quealy, K., and Sanger-Katz, M. "The
Top Jobs Where Women Are Outnumbered by Men
Named John." *New York Times,* April 24, 2018.

p. 181 In fact, of the 20,000+ directors

Eavis, P. "Diversity Push Barely Budges Corporate Boards to 12.5%, Survey Finds." *New York Times,* September 15, 2020.

p. 184 It seems absurd

web.mit.edu/bentley/www/papers/phonebook-CHI15.pdf; www.pewresearch.org/fact-tank/2014/02/03/what-people-like-dislike-about-facebook.

p. 187 Case in point: In April 2018

Meyer, Z. "Starbucks racial-bias training will be costly." *USA Today,* May 29, 2018.

p. 188 In two separate incidents in 2015

B.R. "Nothing to fear except fear itself—Southwest Airlines accused of profiling Muslims." *Economist,* November 23, 2015; Gambino, L. "Southwest Airlines criticized after incidents involving Middle Eastern passengers." *Guardian* (US news), November 21, 2015; "College Student Is Removed From Flight After Speaking Arabic on Plane." *New York Times,* April 17, 2016.

p. 188 Black passengers using ride-sharing

Brown, A. E. *Ridehail Revolution: Ridehail Travel and Equity in Los Angeles.* UCLA, 2018.

p. 188 A study at Harvard

Edelman, Benjamin, Michael Luca, and Dan Svirsky. 2017. "Racial Discrimination in the Sharing Economy: Evidence from a Field Experiment." *American Economic Journal: Applied Economics,* 9, 2, 1–22.

p. 190 When Honda was getting ready

"Lost in Translation: Honda Jazz not Fitta for Scandinavia" (December 17, 2015). Retrieved 11/14/20 from www.originsinfo.com.au.

p. 190   A study from the Kellogg School of Management

Chun, B. "Better Decisions Through Diversity" (October 1, 2010). Retrieved 11/14/20, from insight.kellogg.northwestern.edu.

p. 194   And, in strictly business measures

From Consumers to Creators: The Digital Lives of Black Consumers. Diverse Intelligence Series. Nielsen Company, 2018; Morse, P. "Council Post: Six Facts About the Hispanic Market That May Surprise You." *Forbes*, January 9, 2018.

p. 194   In 2003, scientists sent

Bertrand, Marianne, and Sendhil Mullainathan. "Are Emily and Greg More Employable Than Lakisha and Jamal? A Field Experiment on Labor Market Discrimination." *American Economic Review, 94*, 4 (2004) 991–1013.

p. 196   A 2008 study out of Brandeis

Leslie Zebrowitz, Benjamin White, and Kristin Wieneke. "Mere Exposure and Racial Prejudice: Exposure to Other-Race Faces Increases Liking for Strangers of That Race." *Social Cognition, 26* (2008), 259–75.

p. 196   Another study from the University of Wisconsin

Haq, H. "Can a TV sitcom reduce anti-Muslim bigotry?" *Christian Science Monitor*, January 30, 2016.

p. 196   Other studies from the University of Minnesota

Edward Schiappa, Peter Gregg, and Dean Hewes. "Can One TV Show Make a Difference? Will and Grace and the Parasocial Contact Hypothesis." *Journal of Homosexuality, 51* (2006), 15–37; E. Schiappa, P. B. Gregg, and D. E. Hewes. "Can a Television Series Change Attitudes About Death? A Study of College Students and Six Feet Under." *Death Studies, 28*, 5 (June 2004), 459–74.

p. 200 In what has to be near the top

Martin, L. J., Hathaway, G., Isbester, K., Mirali, S., et al. Reducing social stress elicits emotional contagion of pain in mouse and human strangers. *Current Biology*, *25*, 3 (2015), 326–32.

p. 201 As lead researcher Jeffrey Mogil noted

[McGill University.] "The secret of empathy: Stress from the presence of strangers prevents empathy, in both mice and humans." ScienceDaily, January 15, 2015.

p. 202 Researcher Katherine W. Phillips's group

Katherine W. Phillips, Katie A. Liljenquist, and Margaret A. Neale. "Is the Pain Worth the Gain? The Advantages and Liabilities of Agreeing with Socially Distinct Newcomers." *Personality and Social Psychology Bulletin*, *35* (2009), 336–50.

CHAPTER 7—INFORMATION GATHERING: STAYING CURIOUS IN THE CLUTTER

p. 208 A 2019 neural imaging study

Kenji Kobayashi and Ming Hsu. Common neural code for reward and information value. *Proceedings of the National Academy of Sciences*, *116*, 26 (June 2019), 13061–66.

p. 208 "And just as our brains like"

[University of California—Berkeley Haas School of Business.] "How information is like snacks, money, and drugs—to your brain: Researchers demonstrate common neural code for information and money; both act on the brain's dopamine-producing reward system." ScienceDaily, June 19, 2019.

p. 209 According to the International Data Corporation

Reinsel, D., Gantz, J., and Rydning, J. (2018). *The Digitization of the World From Edge to Core*. www.seagate.com/files/www-content/our-story/trends/files/idc-seagate-dataage-whitepaper.pdf.

p. 209 Data solutions platform NodeGraph

Huchinson, A. "What Happens on the Internet Every Minute." SocialMediaToday, August 11, 2020.

p. 209 The data included: 200 million emails

How much data is on the internet? (March 26, 2020). Retrieved 11/14/20 from www.nodegraph.se.

p. 211 A research study from Experian

Davis, B. The cost of bad data: Stats (March 28, (2014). Retrieved 11/14/20 from econsultancy.com.

p. 211 A 2018 Gartner Research report

The Costs of Poor Data Quality (2018). Retrieved 11/14/20 from www.anodot.com.

p. 212 In an interview for

Harvard Business Review Tichy, N., and Charan, R. "Speed, Simplicity, Self-Confidence: An Interview with Jack Welch." *Harvard Business Review,* September 1989

p. 212 A multitude of studies have found

A. Bessi, et al. "Trend of Narratives in the Age of Misinformation," *PLoS One 10,* 8 (2015), e0134641; A. Bessi, et al. "Viral Misinformation: The Role of Homophily and Polarization." *Proceedings of the 24th International Conference on World Wide Web Companion* (International World Wide Web Conferences Steering Committee, Florence, Italy, 2015), 355–56; M. Del Vicario, et al. "The Spreading of Misinformation Online." *Proceedings of the National Academy of Science USA, 113,* 3

(2016), 554–59; D. Mocanu, L. Ross, Q. Zhang, M. Karsai, and W. Quattrociocchi. "Collective Attention in the Age of (mis) Information." *Computers in Human Behavior,* *51*(2015), 1198–1204; A. Bessi, et al., "Science vs Conspiracy: Collective Narratives in the Age of Misinformation," *PLoS One 10*, 2 (2015), e0118093. F. Zollo, et al., "Debunking in a World of Tribes" (2015). arXiv.org: 1510.04267.

p. 214 As Edwina Dunn, CEO
"The card up their sleeve." *Guardian,* July 18, 2003.

p. 214 Just one year after the Clubcard
Ibid.

p. 215 A survey of over eleven thousand
"Tesco voted the worst supermarket in the UK: Stores given poor marks in pricing, customer service and fresh produce quality in annual poll." *Daily Mail,* February 19, 2013.

p. 215 As profits fell, Tesco
Ahmed, K. "Tesco: Where it went wrong." BBC News, January 19, 2015.

p. 215 In a case described on OneZero
Fry, H. "What Algorithms Know About You Based on Your Grocery Cart" (September 13, 2018). Retrieved 11/14/20 from onezero.medium.com.

p. 217 In an interview with the *Washington Post*
Cole, K. C. "Correlation Is Not Causation." *Washington Post,* March 8, 1995.

p. 217 When it comes to our more complicated
Hopkins, B., and Schadler, T. *Digital Insights Are the New Currency of Business* (2018). Retrieved from www.forrester.com.

p. 218   In a humorous interpretation
www.tylervigen.com/spurious-correlations.

p. 219   But in a clinical trial
NIH stops clinical trial on combination cholesterol treatment. National Institutes of Health (NIH) news release, May 26, 2011.

p. 222   As Ted Sarandos
Adalian, J. "Inside the Binge Factory." *New York Magazine,* June 11, 2018.

p. 228   A classic study
Heider, Fritz, and Marianne Simmel. "An Experimental Study of Apparent Behavior." *The American Journal of Psychology,* 57, 2 (1944), 243–59.

Acknowledgments

I have the deepest gratitude for the opportunities and for all the people who helped me to bring this book into the world.

First and foremost, I want to thank my biological family

To my mom, who was my first teacher, editor, and cheerleader. Thank you for your countless nights of coaching and singing showtunes and loving me unconditionally.

To my dad (Pops), who taught me the love of nature and writing and dreaming. Thank you for loving me not in spite of, but because of, my imperfections.

To my sister, for the years of spinning the spotlight to shine on me and being the wind on which I continue to soar. Thank you for allowing me to fly baby fly.

To David, for your music that I spent nights writing to, your bravery and the reckless abandon with which you embrace all that life has to offer. Thank you for showing me that art is everywhere.

To Warren for your warmth and care of all those you encounter.

To Penny for your passion and advocacy and always being in my corner.

To Cheryl for keeping the family quilted together even when we are physically distant.

To David and Laura, for your unyielding generosity, open arms, and dedication to fighting a bigger common enemy (T1D).

To Craig and Elly, for keeping me healthy, fed, and energized even when my crow experiments were growing in your fridge.

To Oma, for letting me call you Oma, Zoom cocktails, and for empowering women (and being an empowered woman) long before it was cool.

To G'ma Sandy, for her advocacy, strength, and care.

To Lexi, Cam, Dallas, Kristi (Chance and Paxton), for belly laughs and giving me hope for the next generation.

To my cousins, Molly (Ethan), Alex (Melissa), Nathan, Corey, and their children (Matilda and Hayes). I could not have picked better playmates, card sharks, and confidants.

To my grandparents. I miss you every single day.

To Kim whose eyerolls and laughter I still see and hear in my world daily.

To my chosen family

Dermot, you are the love of my life. Thank you for your calm, your patience, and your enduring steady support. You embody the courage, wisdom, and integrity you value. *Tá grá agam duit i gcónaí.*

Connor and Jack, for the debates, discussions, dinners, and keeping your dad sane (for the most part), thank you. It's an honor to be in your life.

Ann and Ian, thank you for accepting me and reminding me to always pause and enjoy the music of a great live concert.

Jenny, my beloved, thank you for rays of thumbs, music, fire, tears, Bird dog days, ceilings, singing, oatmeal mornings, and wine-rich evenings. My life with you is a poem that keeps writing itself and one I never want to finish reading. (Oh, and thank you for all of the countless early edits!)

Shane and Allaine, thank you, thank you, thank you (3x). Allaine, when I grow up, I aspire to have your humor, zest for life, and easygoing kindness. Shane, you are more than you know, and will forever be. Keep that hippie vibe...gurl. Boop.

Patti and Stuart, thank you for sheltering me when I had nowhere to turn. For taking me in, putting me back on my feet, reinvigorating me with purpose, and loving this wayward stranger.

Eileen and Vicki, thank you for teaching me to read, to write, but mostly to love. The two of you have inspired me far beyond any second- or third-grade classroom. Thank you for always believing in me.

And to all of my former students: You all have taught me far more than I was ever able to teach you. The gift of being your teacher has been one of the great honors of my life.

Finally, to those who have poured countless hours directly into making this book a reality

Lucinda Halpern, thank you so much for championing me and this book. To the entire team at Lucinda Literary (especially Connor Eck)—thank you for taking a chance on the unknown kid. I am forever indebted to you.

The incredible editorial consulting of Lisa Sweetingham. I still don't know how you did it, but you found a way to reach into my brain and put the ideas to page in ways my mind would never allow. Thank you for helping my voice translate to something so much stronger than anything I could have produced on my own.

The gurus and experts at Book Highlight, especially Mat Miller and Peter Knox for holding my hand and helping this book reach the right audiences. Your attention at all hours of the day and night made me feel like I was your only client. Thanks for making the Friday phone call always a happy one!

And last but certainly not least, thank you to Denise Silvestro and the entire team at Kensington Books for elevating this non-expert first-timer, and graciously help-ing me navigate the process of publication. It has been a true privilege. To production editor Arthur Maisel, Susan Higgins, my copyeditor, and designer Rachel Reiss, thank you for your care and attention to detail that allowed this book to be interpreted in its most meaningful way. Thanks also to Kristine Noble, the art director, for putting her heart into the cover design and making the jacket pop (and working with the most stubborn of critics—me!). And a huge thank-you to Ann Pryor, marketing director, for helping this book reach the hands of its audience.

KEEP GROWING PAST YOUR INSTINCTS:

Download the **icueity** mobile app to improve your self-awareness and performance with anonymous, 360° feedback from your contacts and colleagues.

icueity

GET CUED IN

Choose from over **90 traits** for assessment and development.

—ACCESS YOUR FREE TRIAL NOW—

icueity is available on the iOS App Store and Google Play

Visit *RebeccaHeiss.com* for more resources, videos, and information.